Practice Book

NATIONAL GEOGRAPHIC
Reach™

Language • Literacy • Content

NATIONAL
GEOGRAPHIC
LEARNING

CENGAGE
Learning·

Contents

Unit 1: Happy to Help

Unit 2: Nature's Balance

Unit 3: Life in the Soil

Unit 4: Let's Work Together

Unit 5: Mysteries of Matter

Unit 6: From Past to Present

Unit 7: Blast! Crash! Splash!

Unit 8: Getting There

Name _____ Date _____

Happy to Help

Make a concept map with the answers to the Big Question: How do people help each other?

How people
help
each other

© National Geographic Learning, a part of Cengage Learning, Inc.

Name _____ Date _____

Someone Who Needs Help

Make a story map about someone you know who needs help.

Beginning:

↓

Middle:

↓

End:

Grammar: Complete Sentences

A Day at the Park

Grammar Rules Complete Sentences

A complete sentence expresses a complete thought. It has a subject and a predicate.

The **subject** tells who or what does something.

The **predicate** tells what the subject does.

The subject usually comes first in a sentence. The predicate usually comes second.

The people | built a nice park.

↑ | ↑

subject | **predicate**

Read each sentence part. Draw a line to match each subject with a predicate.

Subject	Predicate
1. Tanya	a. gather acorns.
2. The birds	b. come to play with Tanya.
3. Two squirrels	c. plays in the park.
4. Some friends	d. shines brightly in the sky.
5. The sun	e. fly from tree to tree.

 Tell a partner how you decided which predicate to match with each subject.

Key Points Reading

Those Shoes

All Jeremy's friends at school have black shoes. Jeremy wants a pair very much.

Jeremy needs a pair of boots for winter. Grandma says they should only buy things that they need.

One day, Jeremy's shoes tear. Jeremy gets shoes with cartoon animals. The kids laugh at his cartoon shoes.

Jeremy and Grandma go to stores that sell old clothes. They look for the black shoes. He finds some, but they are too small. Jeremy buys them anyway. He hopes the shoes will stretch, but they do not. He has to wear the cartoon shoes instead.

Jeremy knows that Antonio needs new shoes. He gives Antonio his black shoes. Jeremy wears the shoes with the cartoon animals. Antonio thanks Jeremy. Jeremy and Antonio become friends.

Name _____ Date _____

Get Well Soon!

Grammar Rules Capital Letters

A complete sentence always begins with a capital letter.

Examples:

Don't write:
my friend needed help.

Write:
My friend needed help.

Circle the letters that should be capitals. Then write the sentences correctly in a paragraph.

> my friend Anna has a cold.
>
> i bring some soup to her house.
>
> she eats the soup.
>
> now she feels better!
>
> her mother thanks me.

_____

_____

_____

_____

_____

_____

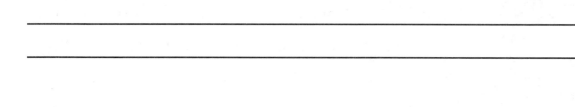 **Tell a partner why you added each capital letter.**

Name _____ Date _____

Vocabulary Bingo

1. Write one Key Word in each shoe.

2. Listen to the clues. Find the Key Word and use a marker to cover it.

3. Say "Bingo!" when you have four markers in a row.

Name _____ Date _____

Those Shoes

Make a story map for "Those Shoes."

┌───┐
│ **Beginning:**   │
│   │
│ First, Jeremy wants new shoes, but they cost │
│ too much.   │
└───┘

↓

┌───┐
│ **Middle:**   │
│   │
│ Next, Jeremy buys shoes that are too   │
│ small.   │
└───┘

↓

┌───┐
│   │
│ Then, _____. │
│   │
│ _____ │
│   │
│ _____ │
│   │
└───┘

↓

┌───┐
│ **End:**   │
│ Finally, _____. │
│   │
│ _____ │
│   │
│ _____ │
└───┘

Use your story map to summarize the story's plot for a partner.

Fluency: Expression

Those Shoes

Use this passage to practice reading with the proper expression.

I have dreams about those shoes. Black high-tops.	8
Two white stripes.	11
"Grandma, I want them."	15
"There's no room for 'want' around here," Grandma says.	24
"What you *need* are new boots for winter."	32

Fluency: Expression

| B | ☐ | Does not read with feeling. | A | ☐ | Reads with appropriate feeling with most content. |
| I | ☐ | Reads with some feeling, but does not match content. | AH | ☐ | Reads with appropriate feeling for all content. |

Accuracy and Rate Formula

Use the formula to measure a reader's accuracy and rate while reading aloud.

$$\underline{\hspace{3cm}} - \underline{\hspace{3cm}} = \underline{\hspace{3cm}}$$

words attempted in one minute	number of errors	words correct per minute (wcpm)

Name _____ Date _____

Guardian Angel

Complete this chart as you read "Guardian Angel."

What I think	What do you think?
Page _____	
_____	
_____	
_____	
Page _____	
_____	
_____	
_____	
Page _____	
_____	
_____	
_____	

 Tell a partner what you would do to help a new student in class feel more welcome.

Name _____ Date _____

Something That Has Improved

Make a comparison chart about something that has improved.

Before	Now

 Tell how you improved something. Tell how the thing was before and how it is now. Use the words *before, then, now,* and *after* to compare.

Grammar: Complete Subjects and Predicates

Soup's On, Kemal!

Grammar Rules Complete Subjects and Predicates

The **complete subject** is all of the words that tell who or what does something.

The **complete predicate** is all of the words that tell what the subject does.

Remember, a sentence always begins with a capital letter.

Example:

A volunteer helps at a soup kitchen.

complete subject   complete predicate

Read each group of words. Combine complete subjects and complete predicates to make sentences. Write the sentences on the lines.

a soup kitchen	tastes good
many individuals	feeds many people
a dish of rice	serve the food

1. _____

2. _____

3. _____

 Talk with a partner about why each complete subject and complete predicate belong together.

© National Geographic Learning, a part of Cengage Learning, Inc.

Key Points Reading

The World's Greatest Underachiever

Henry Winkler wanted to get good grades in school. He studied a lot, but he forgot things easily. He did not give up. He tried to improve his grades.

Henry felt bad about himself. He tried very hard, but people told him he was stupid or lazy.

Henry grew up and became an actor. He also had a son named Jed. Teachers discovered that Jed had dyslexia. This means that his brain learns things in a different way. Then Henry understood that he had dyslexia, too.

Today, Henry talks to other kids about his life. He says to find out what makes you special and share it with the world.

Grammar: Subject-Predicate Agreement

A Helping Paw

Grammar Rules

The **simple subject** is the most important word in the subject. The **simple predicate** is the most important word in the predicate. The simple predicate is often an action word.

When the simple subject is one person or thing and the simple predicate shows action that happens now, the simple predicate ends in -*s*.

Example

The perky <u>dog</u> <u>trots</u> to the door.

When the simple subject is more than one person or thing, the simple predicate that happens now does not end in -*s*.

Example

The happy <u>dogs</u> <u>arrive</u> at the neighborhood hospital.

Read each sentence. Circle the correct form of the simple predicate.

1. A pet owner (take | takes) her dog to visit sick people.
2. The nurses (like | likes) many dogs to visit patients.
3. The friendly dog (place | places) her head next to a patient.
4. A hospital aide (smile | smiles) at the friendly dog.
5. Many relatives (request | requests) visits for their sick family member.

🗨 **Tell your partner how you decided which form of the simple predicate to circle.**

Name _____ Date _____

Compare Henry

Show how Henry changed in "The World's Greatest Underachiever."

Before	Now
1. Henry had trouble spelling.	**1.** Henry writes books.
2. He didn't like school.	**2.**
3.	**3.**
4.	**4.**
5.	**5.**

Use your comparison chart to retell the selection to a partner:
Before, Henry _____. Now, he _____.

Fluency: Intonation

The World's Greatest Underachiever

Use this passage to practice reading with the proper intonation.

The next day, I went into the classroom and took out a sheet of paper.   15

Then Miss Adolf gave us the words. The first word was *carpet*.   27

I wrote that one down: *c-a-r-p-e-t*. I was feeling pretty confident.   38

Then came *neighbor*—I wrote down the letter *n*.   47

Then *rhythm*—I knew there was an *r. Suburban*—I wrote *s-u-b*.   59

My heart sank.   62

I had gone from 100 percent to maybe a D-minus.   72

Where did the words go?   77

Intonation

B ☐ Does not change pitch.   A ☐ Changes pitch to match some of the content.

I ☐ Changes pitch, but does not match content.   AH ☐ Changes pitch to match all of the content.

Accuracy and Rate Formula

Use the formula to measure a reader's accuracy and rate while reading aloud.

$$\underline{\hspace{3cm}} - \underline{\hspace{3cm}} = \underline{\hspace{3cm}}$$

| words attempted in one minute | number of errors | words correct per minute (wcpm) |

Name _____   Date _____

Reading Options: Reflection Journal

Joseph Lekuton: Making a Difference

Complete this chart as you read "Joseph Lekuton: Making a Difference."

Page	Question	Answer

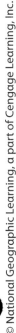

 Work with a small group. Compare your questions and answers with those of other students. Explain how you figured out two of your answers.

Name _____   Date _____

Compare Points of View

Use a comparison chart to compare a biography and an autobiography.

The World's Greatest Underachiever	Joseph Lekuton: Making a Difference
• The narrator tells the story of _____ life.	• The narrator tells the story of _____ life.
• The narrator is/is not part of the story. (Circle one.)	• The narrator is/is not part of the story. (Circle one.)
• The selection is an autobiography/ a biography. (Circle one.)	• The selection is an autobiography/ a biography. (Circle one.)
• Examples of narrator's point of view:	• Examples of narrator's point of view:

 **Take turns with a partner. Describe ways you know that a selection is an autobiography or a biography.**

1.19

Name _____   Date _____

We Like to Read

Grammar Rules Adding -s to Action Verbs

• Use -s at the end of an action verb if the subject is *he, she,* or *it*.	Danny <u>reads</u> a story. He <u>looks</u> at the pictures.
• Do not use -s for *I, you, we,* or *they*.	I <u>read</u> to my friends. They <u>look</u> at the pictures.

Read each sentence. Write the correct form of the verb for each subject.

1. We _____ many stories.
        read/reads

2. I _____ autobiographies.
   like/likes

3. They _____ about real people.
     tell/tells

4. Henry Winkler _____ his own story.
       tell/tells

5. He _____ his problems in school.
   remember/remembers

6. His brain _____ differently.
    learn/learns

7. You _____ autobiographies, too.
   like/likes

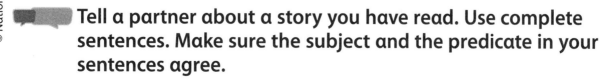 **Tell a partner about a story you have read. Use complete sentences. Make sure the subject and the predicate in your sentences agree.**

© National Geographic Learning, a part of Cengage Learning, Inc.

Name _____ Date _____

The *Be* Verb Game

Grammar Rules Subject-Verb Agreement: *Be*

When you tell what someone or something is now:

- Use **am** after the subject **I**.

  I am helpful.

- Use **is** after the subjects **he**, **she**, and **it**

  He is a volunteer.

- Use **are** after the subjects **you**, **we**, and **they**.

  You are a good neighbor.
  They are good friends.

1. Play with a partner.

2. Spin the spinner.

3. Use the word as a subject. Say a sentence with a *be* verb.

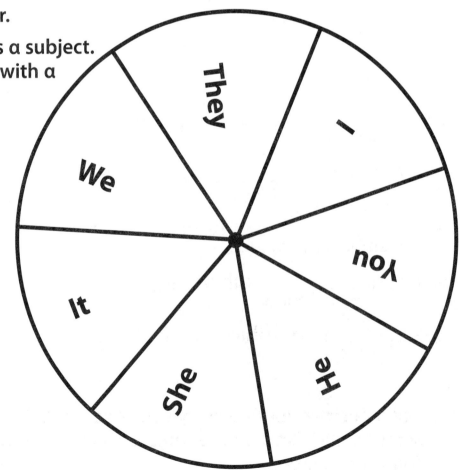

Make a Spinner

1. Push a brad 🖈 through the center of the spinner.

2. Open the brad on the back.

3. Hook a paper clip ⬭ over the brad on the front to make a spinner.

Name _____   Date _____

Voice

Every writer has a special way of saying things, or a voice. The voice should sound genuine, or real, and be unique to that writer.

	Does the writing sound genuine and unique ?	Does the tone fit the audience and purpose?
4	❑ The writing is genuine and unique. It shows who the writer is.	❑ The writer's tone, formal or informal, fits the audience and purpose.
3	❑ Most of the writing sounds genuine and unique.	❑ The writer's tone mostly fits the audience and purpose.
2	❑ Some of the writing sounds genuine and unique.	❑ Some of the writing fits the audience and purpose.
1	❑ The writing does not sound genuine or unique.	❑ The writer's tone does not fit the audience or purpose.

Writing Project: Prewrite

Story Map

Complete the story map for your personal narrative.

> **Beginning:**

> **Middle:**

> **End:**

© National Geographic Learning, a part of Cengage Learning, Inc.

Name _____   Date _____

Revise

Use the Revising Marks to revise this paragraph. Look for:

- a personal voice
- vivid words

Revising Marks	
∧	Add.
ℐ	Take out.
⌒⌐	Move to here.

It was the first day of school. The new girl looked scared.

Another girl went to her and helped her. She showed her to the

right classroom. They ate lunch together. They became friends.

Writing Project

Edit and Proofread

Use the Editing Marks to edit and proofread this paragraph. Look for:

- **complete sentences**
- **capitalization and punctuation**
- **correct spelling**

Editing Marks	
∧	Add.
♪	Take out.
⬭⌒	Move to here.
⬭	Check spelling.
≡	Capitalize.
⊙	Insert period.

I was late to school mom droped me off at the front steps.

I grabbed my bag and ran My bag was open, though, and my

papers spilled all over the ground! I watched them fly in different

directions, and I wanted to cry. Just then Isabella appeared.

scooped up my papers and walked over to me. I was so hapy. She

saved my day!

© National Geographic Learning, a part of Cengage Learning, Inc.

Name _____   Date _____

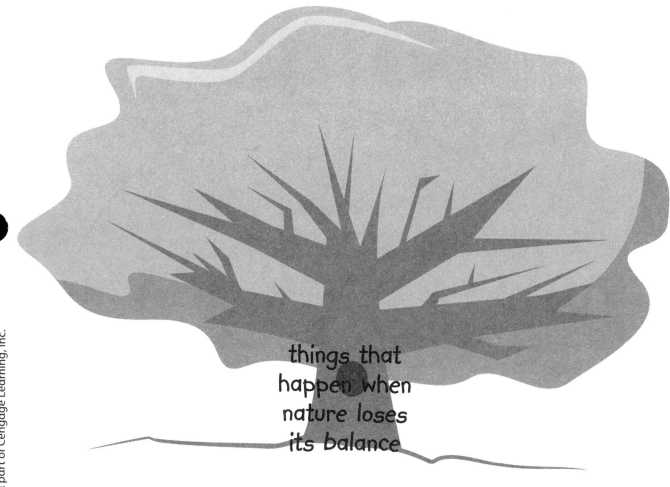

Unit Concept Map

Nature's Balance

Make a concept map with the answers to the Big Question: What happens when nature loses its balance?

things that happen when nature loses its balance

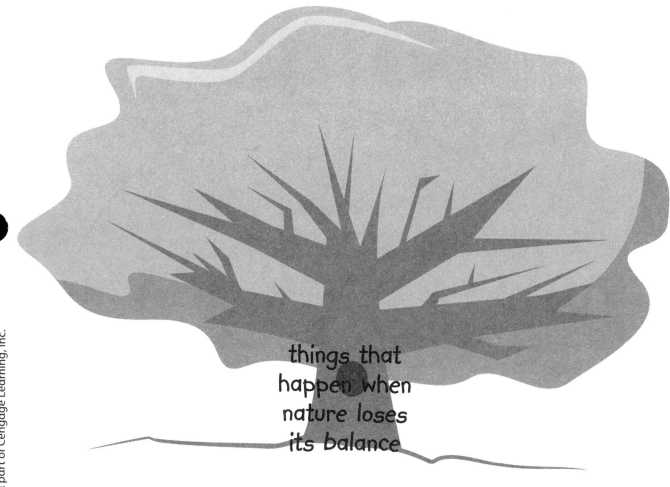

Name _____ Date _____

Comparing Supplies

Compare the two pictures.

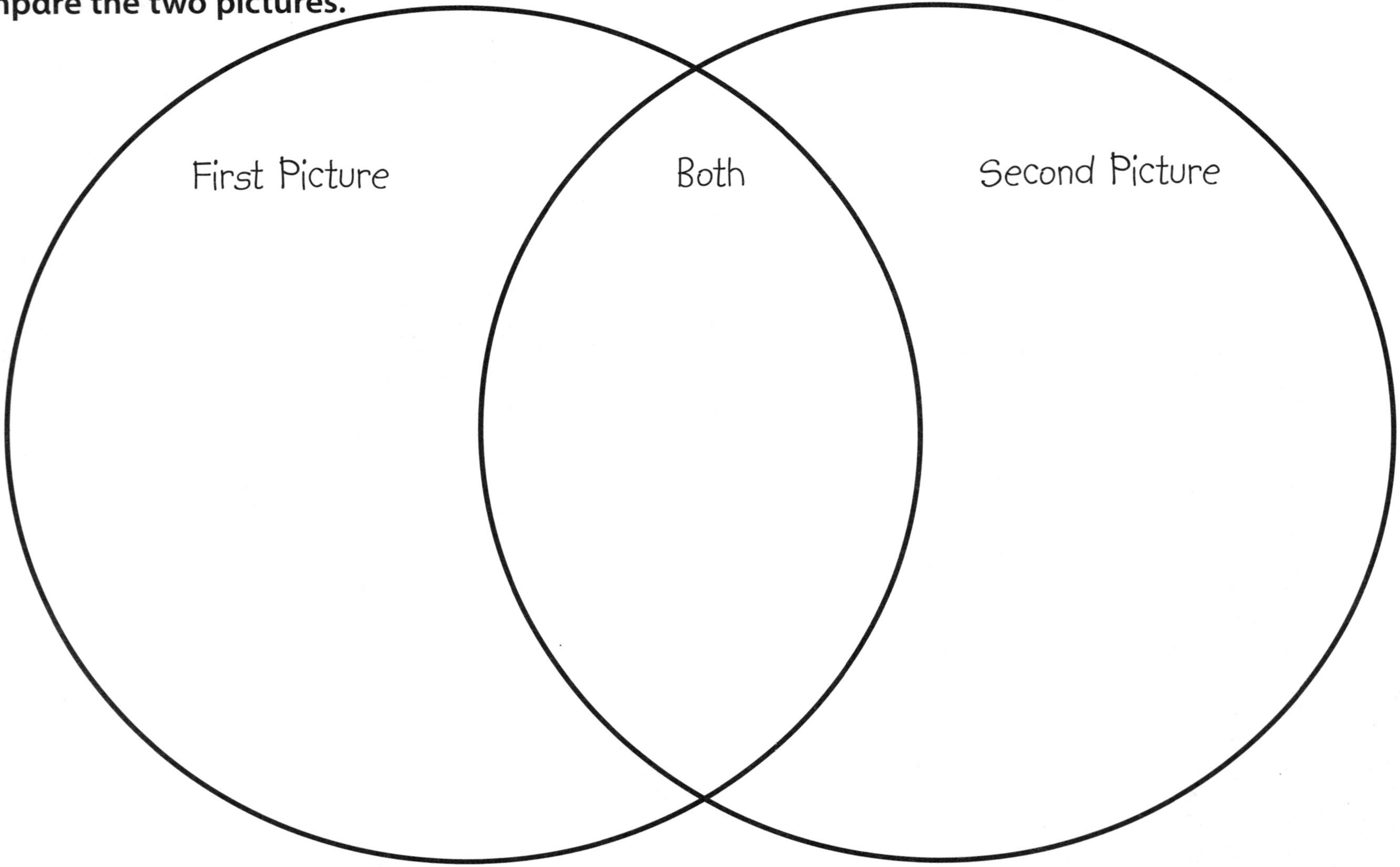

First Picture

Both

Second Picture

Take turns comparing and contrasting two different animals you know about.

For use with TE p. T74a

2.2

Unit 2 | Nature's Balance

Grammar: Kinds of Sentences

The Dog and the Squirrel

Grammar Rules Kinds of Sentences

A **statement** tells something. It ends with a period.	The squirrel eats acorns.
An **exclamation** shows strong feeling. It ends with an exclamation mark.	Its teeth are so sharp!
A **command** tells someone to do something. It ends with a period or an exclamation mark.	Watch it run up the tree. Hurry up and look!

Read each sentence. Write the correct, or the best, end mark in the box. Add S for a statement, E for an exclamation, and C for a command.

1. My dog, Barney, chases squirrels ☐ _____

2. He is so crazy ☐ _____

3. Watch him closely ☐ _____

4. I see a squirrel over there ☐ _____

5. Run, Barney, run ☐ _____

6. Don't worry ☐ _____

7. The squirrels always get away ☐ _____

8. Good job, Barney ☐ _____

Read the sentences to your partner with the correct expression. Pay attention to the punctuation.

Name _____   Date _____

When the Pigs Took Over

Don Carlos is Alonzo's big brother. Don Carlos likes more of everything.

Don Carlos owns a restaurant. Alonzo plays his violin at the restaurant. Don Carlos always asks for more.

Alonzo reads that in a big restaurant in the city people eat snails. Don Carlos and Alonzo get some snails. But Don Carlos wants more!

Soon there are too many snails. So Don Carlos and Alonzo throw small pieces of bread to bring birds to eat the snails.

At first, a few birds come. But Don Carlos wants more! The birds eat all the snails. But now there are too many birds!

Don Carlos and Alonzo bring pigs to chase the birds away. A few pigs are not enough. Don Carlos wants more!

The pigs run everywhere. They eat everything. Alonzo and the villagers play music to chase the pigs away.

Now, Don Carlos knows that more is not always better.

Grammar: Kinds of Sentences

What's the Question?

Grammar Rules Questions

For questions with short answers, use *Who, What, Where,* or *When.*	**What** is your name? My name is Emily.
For yes/no questions, use *Is, Are, Do* and *Does.*	**Are** you in the third grade? Yes, I am. **Do** you speak French? No, I don't.

1. Toss a coin with a partner. Heads moves 1 space. Tails moves 2.

2. Ask your partner a question that starts with the words in the square. Your partner answers the question.

When is ____?	Does our school ____?	Do you ____?	What is ____?
Does a dog ____?			Is today ____?
Where is ____?			**End**
Are these books ____?	Is your name ____?	Who is ____?	**Begin**

▰▰ Ask and answer three questions about school with a partner.

Reread and Compare and Contrast: Venn Diagram

When the Pigs Took Over

Compare Alonzo and Don Carlos.

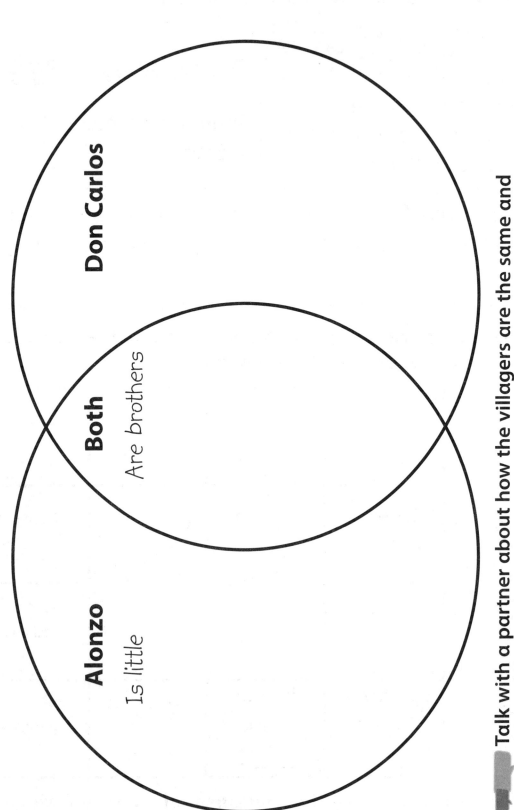

Don Carlos

Both

Are brothers

Alonzo

Is little

Talk with a partner about how the villagers are the same and how they are different.

Name _____   Date _____

Use this passage to practice reading with proper expression.

When the Pigs Took Over

The pigs kept running wild.	5
Don Carlos put his hands over his ears. The music was more	17
than even he could stand. "¡No más!" he cried.	26
"¡Más!" Alonzo shouted to the villagers.	32
The villagers marched through the streets, playing louder	40
and louder.	42

Expression

B ☐ Does not read with feeling.	A ☐ Reads with appropriate feeling for most content.
I ☐ Reads with some feeling, but does not match content.	AH ☐ Reads with appropriate feeling for all content.

Use the formula to measure a reader's accuracy and rate while reading aloud.

Accuracy and Rate Formula

$$\underset{\substack{\text{words attempted} \\ \text{in one minute}}}{\underline{\hspace{4cm}}} - \underset{\text{number of errors}}{\underline{\hspace{4cm}}} = \underset{\substack{\text{words correct per minute} \\ \text{(wcpm)}}}{\underline{\hspace{4cm}}}$$

Name _____ Date _____

Animals, More or Less

Complete this chart as you read "Animals, More or Less."

What I think:	What do you think?
Page _____ _____ _____ _____ _____	_____ _____ _____ _____ _____
Page _____ _____ _____ _____ _____	_____ _____ _____ _____ _____
Page _____ _____ _____ _____ _____	_____ _____ _____ _____ _____

 Tell a partner which riddle you liked the best. Explain why it was funny.

Name _____ Date _____

Compare Genres

Use this chart to compare a humorous story and a riddle.

	Humorous Story	Riddle
funny	✓	✓
usually long		
short		
playful language		
paragraphs		
questions and answers		

 Talk with a partner about which kind of humorous selection you liked better—the story or the riddles. Tell your partner why you liked one more than the other.

Name _____ Date _____

Food for the Birds

Grammar Rules Kinds of Sentences

A **statement** tells something.	I have a pet bird.
An **exclamation** shows strong feeling.	He is so funny!
A **command** tells someone to do something.	Look at this picture of him.
A **question** asks something.	Do you have a pet?
Sometimes the answer to a question has a **contraction**.	No, I **don't**. No, it **isn't**.

Read each sentence. Write C for command, S for statement, E for exclamation, and Q for question. Then underline the contractions.

1. Do you like corn? _____

2. No, I don't. _____

3. I really love corn! _____

4. Some birds like it, too. _____

5. Where do they find corn? _____

6. Look at the bird feeder. _____

7. Wow! It's full of corn! _____

 Write a statement, a question, and an exclamation about something that happened today. Read your sentences to your partner.

Name _____ Date _____

Thinking Map: Cause-and-Effect Diagram

Ecosystem Alert

Make a cause-and-effect diagram of an ecosystem that is out of balance.

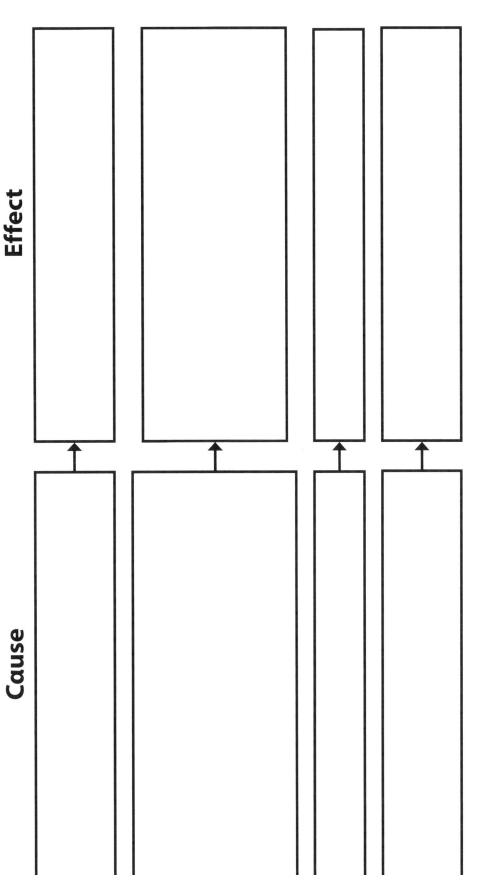

Cause

Effect

Use your chart to tell a partner about one cause and its effect shown on page 105.

Name _____   Date _____

All About Bears

Grammar Rules Compound Sentences

You can make a compound sentence by joining two short sentences. Use a comma + joining word (*and, but, or*).

> Bears eat berries, **and** they also eat fish.
>
> An adult bear is very tall, **but** a baby bear is much smaller.
>
> Bears can walk on four legs, **or** they can walk on two legs.

Combine each pair of sentences into one compound sentence. Use the joining word in ( ).

1. Bears look cute. They are dangerous. (but)

_____

2. You can see bears in a zoo. You might see one in the woods. (or)

_____

3. Bears catch fish in their paws. They eat as many as they can. (and)

_____

4. It is fun to see wild animals. Don't go too close to them. (but)

_____

 Tell a partner about two kinds of animals you know about. Use some compound sentences.

Name _____   Date _____

When the Wolves Returned

Yellowstone Park is a very special place in northwestern Wyoming. It has more natural wonders than any other place on Earth.

Many animals live in Yellowstone. There are elk, deer, and wolves. People liked seeing the elk and deer, but the wolves ate many of these animals.

The people that ran the park gave money to hunters to kill the wolves. They did not know that this would change many things.

Without the wolves, there were too many elk and coyotes. Because there were too many coyotes, other animals started to disappear. Many animals could not find food or places to live.

Scientists said that the problems started when the wolves left Yellowstone. They brought back the wolves.

Now, the other animals are surviving. They have food and places to live. Yellowstone is a balanced ecosystem again.

Grammar: Compound Sentences

Spin a Sentence

Grammar Rules Compound Sentences: Coordinating Conjunctions

Use *and* to join ideas that are alike.

Use *but* to join ideas that show a difference.

Use *or* to show a choice.

1. Play with a partner.

2. Spin the spinner. Read the sentence.

3. Add another idea that is alike, different, or shows a choice. Use *and, but,* or *or* to make a compound sentence.

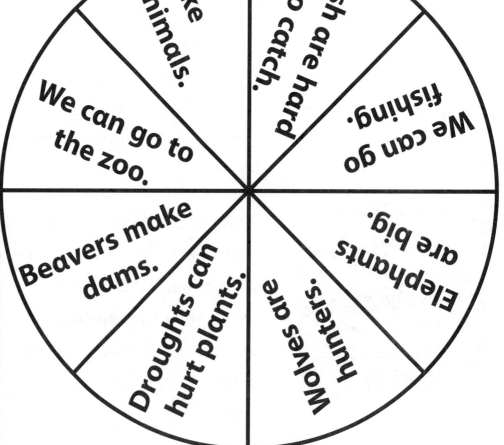

I like animals.

Fish are hard to catch.

We can go to the zoo.

We can go fishing.

Beavers make dams.

Elephants are big.

Droughts can hurt plants.

Wolves are hunters.

Make a Spinner

1. Push a brad ⋏ through the center of the spinner.

2. Open the brad on the back.

3. Hook a paper clip ⊂▭⊃ over the brad on the front to make a spinner.

Name _____   Date _____

Reread and Retell: Cause-and-Effect Diagram

When the Wolves Returned

Complete this chart as you reread "When the Wolves Returned."

Cause		Effect
Park officials got rid of the wolves.	→	The number of elk increased.
Coyotes became the main predators in the park.	→	
	→	
	→	
	→	

© National Geographic Learning, a part of Cengage Learning, Inc.

 Tell a partner about causes and effects in the selection that surprised you.

Fluency: Phrasing

Use this passage to practice reading with proper phrasing.

When the Wolves Returned

The purpose for making Yellowstone a national park was to	10
protect its natural wonders for visitors. People enjoyed seeing	19
animals in the park, too, like elk and deer. But wolves fed on	32
them. So, hunters were paid to kill the wolves. Park officials did	44
not understand that killing the wolves would throw nature out	54
of balance.	56

Phrasing

B ☐ Rarely pauses while reading the text.   A ☐ Frequently pauses at appropriate points in the text.

I ☐ Occasionally pauses while reading the text.   AH ☐ Consistently pauses at all appropriate points in the text.

Accuracy and Rate Formula

Use the formula to measure a reader's accuracy and rate while reading aloud.

_____ - _____ = _____
words attempted   number of errors   words correct per minute
in one minute   (wcpm)

Name _____ Date _____

Reading Options: Reflection Journal

Megafish Man

Complete this chart as you read "Megafish Man."

Page	My question	The answer

💬 **Tell a partner which answer or fact was most interesting and why.**

Name _____ Date _____

Compare Ecosystems

Compare Yellowstone Park and the Mekong River.

Yellowstone Park	Mekong River
Is in the United States	Is in Cambodia

 Tell your partner which ecosystem you would rather visit and why.

Grammar: Compound Sentences

Pets for Aziz

Grammar Rules Compound Sentences

You can use *and*, *but*, or *or* to combine two short sentences into one long compound sentence.

1. Use *and* to join ideas that are alike.

   Dogs are friendly, **and** *they make good pets.*

2. Use *or* to join ideas that are different.

   Dogs like to be with people, **but** *cats often like to be alone.*

3. Use *or* to join ideas that show a choice.

   You might like to have a dog, **or** *you might rather have a cat.*

Use *and*, *but* or *or* to complete each compound sentence.

Aziz loves animals, ____*and*____ he has several pets. His dog sleeps

in the kitchen, _____ his two cats sleep there too. Some dogs

and cats fight each other, _____ his play together every day.

Aziz wants to get a snake, _____ maybe he would choose

a lizard instead. He asked his mother to buy a snake for him,

_____ she said no. She doesn't like snakes, _____ she doesn't

want another pet. Maybe Aziz should ask again, _____ maybe

he should just visit the zoo!

💬 **Tell a partner about different kinds of pets. Use compound sentences.**

© National Geographic Learning, a part of Cengage Learning, Inc.

Name _____   Date _____

Ideas

Writing is well-developed when the message is clear and interesting to the reader. It is supported by details that show the writer knows the topic well.

	Is the message clear and interesting?	Do the details show the writer knows the topic?
4	❑ All of the writing is clear and focused. ❑ The writing is very interesting.	❑ All the details tell about the topic. The writer knows the topic well.
3	❑ Most of the writing is clear and focused. ❑ Most of the writing is interesting.	❑ Most of the details are about the topic. The writer knows the topic fairly well.
2	❑ Some of the writing is not clear. The writing lacks some focus. ❑ Some of the writing is confusing.	❑ Some details are about the topic. The writer doesn't know the topic well.
1	❑ The writing is not clear or focused. ❑ The writing is confusing.	❑ Many details are not about the topic. The writer does not know the topic.

Name _____ Date _____

Cause-and-Effect Diagram

Use this cause-and-effect diagram to list the important ideas for your summary.

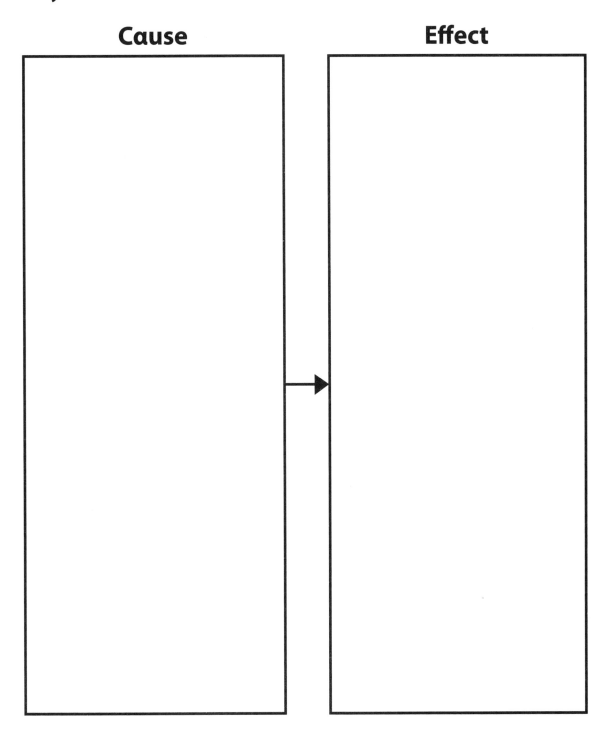

Cause

Effect

Name ______________________ Date ______________

Writing Project

Revise

Use the Revising Marks to revise this paragraph. Look for:

- **information that doesn't tell about the topic**
- **information that tells about the beginning, middle, and end of the selection**

Revising Marks	
^	Add.
	Take out.
	Move to here.

Park officials hired hunters to kill wolves at Yellowstone National Park because the wolves were killing the other animals. Yellowstone is in northwestern Wyoming. Killing the wolves created a problem no one had counted on. The number of coyotes and elk grew out of control. They destroyed the trees and shrubs that birds and beavers need to survive. They ate animals that other animals needed for food. Elk are one of the largest animals in North America.

Writing Project

Edit and Proofread

Use the Editing Marks to edit and proofread this paragraph. Look for:

- **correct compound sentences**
- **correct contractions**

Editing Marks	
∧	Add.
⤴	Take out.
⬭⤴	Move to here.
⤴	Insert comma.
⤸	Insert apostrophe.

Park officials in Yellowstone did'nt used to think wolves in the

park were useful but now they do. In 1926, the last wolves in the

park were killed. The number of elk increased. Park rangers had

to trap them or they had to hunt them. The number of coyotes

also increased and they ate food other animals needed. Scientists

realized theyd made a mistake, so they brought wolves back into

Yellowstone. The officials willn't let the ecosystem get unbalanced

again.

Life in the Soil

Make a concept map with the answers to the Big Question: What is so amazing about plants?

amazing things about plants

Name _____   Date _____

Thinking Map: Sequence Chain

Steps in a Plant's Life

Make a sequence chain of a plant's life.

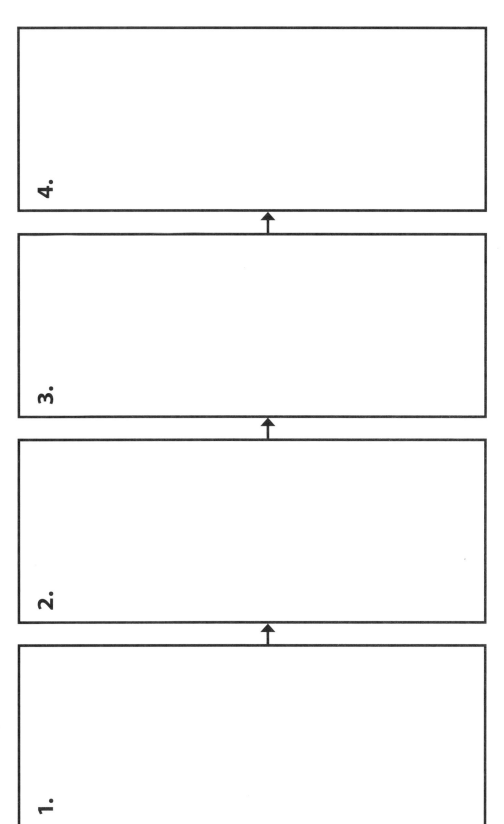

1.

2.

3.

4.

Grammar: Plural Nouns with -s and -es

Too Many Rose Blossoms!

Grammar Rules Plural Nouns

1. To make plural forms of many nouns, add -s.

      sprout → sprout<u>s</u>   day → day<u>s</u>

2. To make plural forms of nouns that end in *x, ch, sh, ss, z,* and sometimes *o,* add -es.

      inch → inch<u>es</u>   potato → potato<u>es</u>

3. To make plural forms of nouns that end in a consonant and then *y,* change the *y* to *i,* and add -es.

      baby → bab<s>y</s> *i* + *es* = bab<u>ies</u>

Fix each mistake. Write the plural form of each underlined noun.

1. My family likes rose <u>garden</u> a lot! _____

2. We visited two <u>city</u> with rose gardens last week. _____

3. One city garden had 20 different kinds of rose <u>bush</u>! _____

4. Each rose bush had too many <u>blossom</u> to count. _____

5. We met two other <u>family</u> that like rose gardens, too. _____

6. They said they had visited 10 rose gardens in two <u>day</u>. _____

    Use two of the plural nouns above. Tell a partner about a plant you have seen.

3.3

Name _____   Date _____

Two Old Potatoes and Me

A girl finds two old potatoes. The potatoes have sprouts growing from their eyes. Her dad says new potatoes can grow from the old ones. The girl and her dad take the potatoes to the garden. They plant pieces of the potatoes with the eyes facing up.

In May, little green plants poke out of the soil. In June, little violet flowers grow on the plants. In July, the plants grow tall. In August, the leaves turn brown, but the plants are not dead. Potatoes are growing under the ground.

In September, the girl and her dad dig up the potatoes. The girl counts sixty-seven potatoes! Finally, the girl and her dad eat mashed potatoes together. Yum!

Grammar: Nouns and Articles

Day in the Park

Grammar Rules Nouns and Articles

1. Use *a* or *an* to talk about something in general.
   Before a noun that starts with a consonant sound, use *a*.

         a plant   a garden   a person

   Before a noun that starts with a vowel sound, use *an*.

         an ant   an idea   an ocean

2. Use *the* to talk about something specific.

         the boy next door   the plant by my window

Add the correct article before each noun.

On Saturday, I had _____ idea for a fun day! _____ friend and I walked to Hunters Park. We like _____ park a lot. We saw many beautiful plants in _____ garden there. We saw _____ orchid and _____ rose. We saw _____ animal in _____ park, too. It was a great day in _____ park!

> **Use each of the three articles in sentences. Tell a partner about a place you like.**

Vocabulary Bingo

1. Write one Key Word in each leaf.

2. Listen to the clues. Find the Key Word and use a marker to cover it.

3. Say "Bingo" when you have four markers in a row.

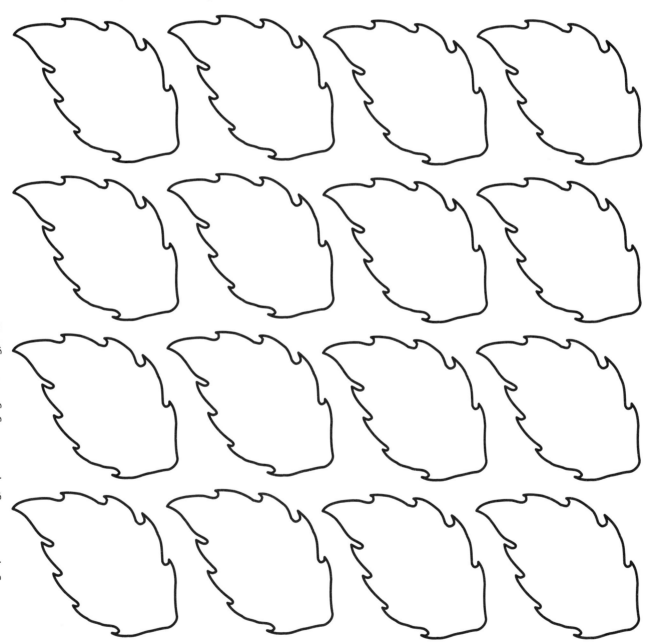

Reread and Retell: Sequence Chain

Two Old Potatoes and Me

Make a sequence chain of "Two Old Potatoes and Me."

1. A girl finds two potatoes with sprouts.

2. She and her dad plant them.

3.

4.

5.

6.

7.

💬 **Use your sequence chain to retell the story to a partner.**

© National Geographic Learning, a part of Cengage Learning, Inc.

Fluency: Expression

Two Old Potatoes and Me

Use this passage to practice reading with proper expression.

"Gross." I tossed them in the trash.   7

"Wait," Dad said. "I think we can grow new potatoes with those.   19

I'll call your grandpa. He'll know."   25

Dad and I talked with Grandpa. The we took the potatoes to the   38

sunniest spot in the garden.   43

Expression

B ☐ Does not read with feeling.   A ☐ Reads with appropriate feeling for some content.

I ☐ Reads with feeling, but does not match content.   AH ☐ Reads with appropriate feeling for all content.

Accuracy and Rate Formula

Use the formula to measure a reader's accuracy and rate while reading aloud.

_____ − _____ = _____
words attempted   number of errors   words corrected per
in one minute   minute (wcpm)

Name _____ Date _____

America's Sproutings

Complete this chart as you read "America's Sproutings."

Page	What I read	What it means to me

Tell a partner which poem was your favorite and why.

Name _____   Date _____

Respond and Extend: Venn Diagram

Compare Genres

Compare a story and a haiku.

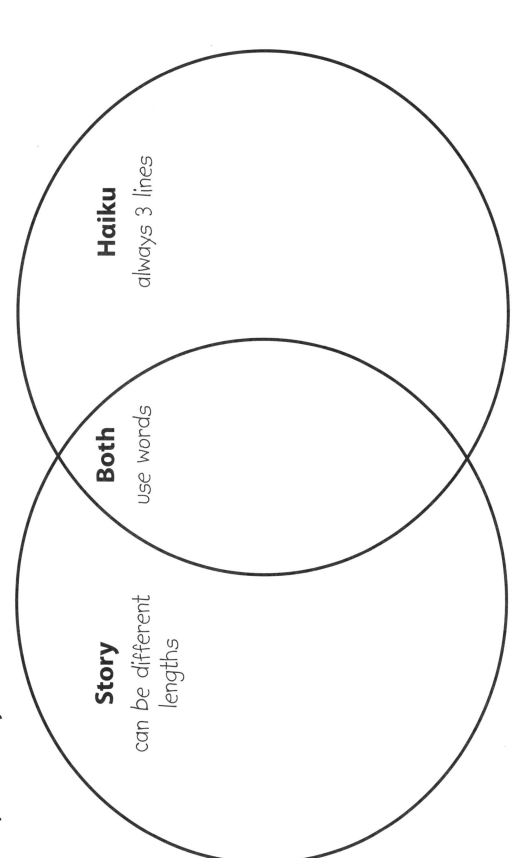

Story
can be different lengths

Both
use words

Haiku
always 3 lines

Take turns with a partner. Ask each other questions about a story or haiku.

Name _____   Date _____

Strange Garden Plants

Grammar Rules Plural Nouns

1. To make many nouns plural, add -s to the end.

   sprout → sprout<u>s</u>

2. For nouns that end in x, ch, sh, ss, z, and some that end in o, add -es.

   branch → branch<u>es</u>   fox → fox<u>es</u>

3. For nouns that end in a consonant plus y, change the y to i and add -es. For nouns that end with a vowel plus y, just add -s.

   cherry → cherr<u>ies</u>   boy → boy<u>s</u>

Write the plural nouns.

My grandmother has a strange garden. She has ___*boxes*___ full of
(box)
_____ all over her deck. She has _____ of _____ growing
(sprout)   (bunch)   (daisy)
in old boots, and _____ in coffee cans. Colored _____ make
(lily)   (glass)
pretty vases. They line her windowsills. _____ curl around her
(Vine)
garden swings and _____ . She also made strange metal
(bench)
_____ . She stuck them in the ground between the _____ .
(flower)   (bush)
Yes, her garden is odd. I love the _____ I spend there.
(day)

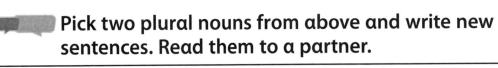

💬 **Pick two plural nouns from above and write new
sentences. Read them to a partner.**

Thinking Map: Main Idea and Details Diagram

Main Idea and Details

Make a main idea and details diagram for rainforest plants.

```
┌─────────────────────────────────┐
│                                 │
│                                 │
│                                 │
└──────────┬──────────────────────┘
           │  1.                   │
           │                       │
           ├───────────────────────┤
           │  2.                   │
           │                       │
           ├───────────────────────┤
           │  3.                   │
           │                       │
           └───────────────────────┘
```

 Tell the main idea about rainforest plants and the two details that you find most interesting.

 © National Geographic Learning, a part of Cengage Learning, Inc.

Grammar: Plural Nouns, Count and Noncount

The Perfect Rainforest Animal

Grammar Rules Count and Noncount Nouns

Some nouns name things that can be counted. These nouns have a singular form and a plural form.

papaya → papayas   cloud → clouds   game → games

Some nouns name things that cannot be counted. These nouns have only one form.

milk   food   snow   sunlight   rain

Fill in each blank with the correct form of the noun.

1. Okapis are perfect _____ for the rainforest.
(animal)

2. The _____ that falls every day slides off the okapi's fur.
(rain)

3. Shadows and _____ create light and dark places.
(sunlight)

4. An okapi's stripes blend in with the _____.
(sunlight)

5. Male okapis have short _____.
(horn)

6. Short _____ do not get caught in the vines and bushes.
(horn)

7. Okapi mothers produce a lot of _____ for their babies.
(milk)

8. Adult okapis get all the _____ they need from the rainforest.
(food)

Use two of the nouns above. Tell a partner something you know about the kind of weather you like.

A Protected Place

The Okapi Reserve

The Okapi Reserve is a tropical rainforest in the Congo. It has a lot of plants that do not grow anywhere else. The people that started the reserve wanted to protect many different plants and animals.

A Home for Animals and Humans

These are some of the animals that live in the reserve. Some of the animals live on the ground. Some of them live in the trees. People live on the reserve, too.

A Brave Man

Corneille Ewango is a scientist. He works on the reserve. He loves the forest and its plants and animals. He believes that more scientists and young people should understand the rainforests in the Congo.

Grammar: Common and Proper Nouns

People of the Reserve

Grammar Rules Common and Proper Nouns

1. A common noun names any person, place, thing, or idea. A common noun starts with a lowercase letter.

2. A proper noun names a particular person, place, or thing. A proper noun starts with a capital letter.

3. A short way to write a person's title starts with a capital letter and ends with a period.

	Common Noun	Proper Noun
Person	man	Mr. Ewango
Place	country	Congo
Thing	forest	Ituri Forest

Circle the common or proper noun that belongs in each blank.

1. People live in _____ in many parts of the world. (rainforests/Ituri Forest)

2. The _____ are a special group of people. (people/Mbuti Pygmies)

3. They live in the Okapi Reserve in the _____. (country/Congo)

4. The people, plants, and animals of the _____ were once in danger. (reserve/Okapi Reserve)

5. _____ and other people are working to save the Okapi Reserve. (A scientist/Mr. Ewango)

© National Geographic Learning, a part of Cengage Learning, Inc.

A Protected Place

Make a main idea and details diagram for "A Protected Place."

> Main Idea:
> The Okapi Reserve is an amazing place, full of amazing plants.

> Supporting Detail:
>
>
> Supporting Detail:
>
>
>
>
>
>

Name _____   Date _____

A Protected Place

Use this passage to practice reading with proper phrasing.

They understand everything about the forest, and they rely on it   11

for food, shelter, and clothing.   16

Pygmies travel from place to place to hunt and fish.   26

They don't just catch game, though.   32

They also collect insects, seeds, fruit, and honey to eat.   42

Phrasing

B ☐ Consistent pauses to match appropriate phrasing.   A ☐ Occasional pauses that match appropriate phrasing.

I ☐ Frequent pauses that match appropriate phrasing.   AH ☐ Rare pauses at appropriate points in text.

Accuracy and Rate Formula

Use the formula to measure a reader's accuracy and rate while reading aloud.

_____ − _____ = _____
words attempted   number of errors   words correct per
in one minute   minute (wcpm)

Name _____   Date _____

Rosie's Reports

Complete this sheet as you read "Rosie's Reports."

An amazing fact about _____

is _____.

An amazing fact about _____

is_____.

An amazing fact about _____

is_____.

The most amazing fact of all is _____.

 Tell a partner which fact was most amazing. Explain why you think it is.

Respond and Extend: Comparison Chart

Compare Text Features

Compare "A Protected Place" and "Rosie's Reports."

"A Protected Place"	"Rosie's Reports"
Feature: Captions Example: An okapi runs through the woods.	Feature: Captions Example: A worker gets ready to wrap a bundle of leaves.
	Feature: Date line Example: Date: November 8

 Take turns with a partner. Ask each other questions about the blog and the article.

Name _____   Date _____

The Make-It-Plural Game

Grammar Rules More Plural Nouns

Add -s or -es to make most nouns plural:

plant → plants   box → boxes   baby → babies

For a few nouns, use special forms to show the plural:

leaf → leaves   foot → feet   man → men

woman → women   child → children

1. **Play with a partner.**

2. **Spin the spinner.**

3. **Change the noun to a plural noun. Say a sentence using the plural noun.**

Make a Spinner

1. Push a brad 𝍏 through the center of the spinner.

2. Open the brad on the back.

3. Hook a paper clip ⊂⊃ over the brad on the front to make a spinner.

(Spinner with words: leaf, fork, fox, flower, child, foot, woman, party)

© National Geographic Learning, a part of Cengage Learning, Inc.

Writing Project: Rubric

Ideas

Every writer has a special way of saying things, or a voice. The voice should sound genuine, or real, and be unique to that writer.

	Is the message clear and interesting?	Do the details show the writer knows the topic?
4	❏ All of the writing is clear and focused. ❏ The writing is very interesting.	❏ All the details tell about the topic. The writer knows the topic well.
3	❏ Most of the writing is clear and focused. ❏ Most of the writing is interesting.	❏ Most of the details are about the topic. The writer knows the topic fairly well.
2	❏ Some of the writing is not clear. The writing lacks some focus. ❏ Some of the writing is confusing.	❏ Some details are about the topic. The writer doesn't know the topic well.
1	❏ The writing is not clear or focused. ❏ The writing is confusing.	❏ Many details are not about the topic. The writer does not know the topic.

Writing Project: Prewrite

Main Idea and Details Diagram

Complete the main idea and details diagram for your article.

Main Idea:

↓

Supporting Detail:

↓

Supporting Detail:

↓

Supporting Detail:

© National Geographic Learning, a part of Cengage Learning, Inc.

Writing Project

Revise

Use the Revising Marks to revise this paragraph. Look for:
- **a topic sentence**
- **sentence variety**

Revising Marks	
^	Add.
ℛ	Take out.
⬭⌃	Move to here.
⬭	Check spelling.

   Trees are all along the city streets. Grass covers the fields in

the park. Flowers are in pots next to the stores. Weeds even grow

through cracks in the sidewalk

● **Writing Project**

Edit and Proofread

Use the Editing Marks to edit and proofread this paragraph. Look for:
- **correct spelling of plural nouns**
- **indenting**
- **correct articles**

Editing Marks	
∧	Add.
℘	Take out.
⬭⤻	Move to here.
⬭	Check spelling.
⌐	Indent.

Plants can grow to be many different sizes. Pansys might be just an

few inchs. In the desert, a Saguaro cactus can grow to about 40 feet

tall. The redwood tree can be over 300 foots tall! It is amazing how

many different sizes plantes can be.

Name _____   Date _____

Let's Work Together

Make a concept map with the answers to the Big Question: What's the best way to get things done?

What's the best way to get things done?

Name _____   Date _____

Thinking Map: Theme Chart

Make a theme chart about your partner's story.

Title: _____

Theme Chart

Clues from the Title:	Clues from the Characters:

Theme:

Clues from the Setting:	Clues from the Events:

Discuss the clues in the theme chart with a partner. Does your partner agree with the clues you listed?

Name _____ Date _____

Food Drive

Grammar Rules Present-Tense Action Verbs

A present-tense action verb tells what happens now or what happens often. If the subject of the sentence tells about one other person or thing, add **-s** to the end of most action verbs. For other subjects, do not add **-s**.

Tony **buys** eggs.

His sisters **buy** milk.

Fill in the blanks with present-tense action verbs.

Many families need help. Our teacher _____ a food drive
(lead)

to help families. First, Ms. Garcia _____ an advertisement
(write)

about it. Then students _____ canned food from home.
(bring)

Briana _____ the food. Carlos _____ it. Then our teacher
(collect)   (sort)

_____ the food to a local food bank. Many helpers _____
(take)   (work)

together to accomplish something good.

 Tell a partner how students at your school work together on a project. Use present-tense action verbs.

Key Points Reading

Mama Panya's Pancakes

Mama Panya is going to make pancakes. She and Adika go to the market to buy what they need. Adika asks what they will buy. Mama Panya says "A little bit and a little bit more."

On the way, Adika asks five friends to have pancakes with them. Mama Panya is worried there won't be enough for everyone. But Adika says "You'll have a little bit and a little bit more. That's enough."

At the market, Mama Panya buys flour and a chili pepper for the pancakes. Adika asks each seller to eat pancakes with them. They give more flour and a larger chili pepper to Mama Panya. But she is still worried that there will not be enough for everyone.

Adika tells her not to worry. He says they have a little bit and a little bit more.

That evening, all of Mama Panya's and Adika's friends come to their house for pancakes. Everyone brings some food to share.

Mama Panya is very happy! Adika says that he knows she wants to make pancakes again soon.

Grammar: Present Tense

Sentence Match

Grammar Rules Present Tense

The verbs *am, is,* and *are* can link the subject of a sentence to a word in the predicate. *Am, is* and *are* are forms of the verb *be*.

Fill in each blank with the correct form of the verb *be*. Then check with a partner. Do your sentences match?

1. I _____ happy at the party.

2. He _____ happy at the party.

3. They _____ ready to play games.

4. She _____ good at playing dodge ball.

5. You _____ nine years old today.

6. I _____ still eight years old.

7. I _____ his neighbor.

8. We _____ best friends.

 Pretend that you are at a party. Talk with a partner about it. Use sentences with *am, is,* and *are*.

4.5

Reread and Paraphrase: Theme Chart

Mama Panya's Pancakes

Make a theme chart of "Mama Panya's Pancakes."

Theme Chart

Clues from the Title:	Clues from the Characters:
"Mama Panya's Pancakes" makes me think the story is about food.	

Theme:

Clues from the Setting:	Clues from the Events:

 Compare your theme sentence with a partner's sentence. Can both themes apply to the story? Discuss.

Mama Panya's Pancakes

Use this passage to practice reading with proper intonation.

Adika popped up. "Mama's making pancakes today. Can you come?"   10

"Oh, how wonderful! I think we can give a little more for that coin."   24

Bwana Zawenna put more flour on the paper, then tied it up with string.   38

"We'll see you later."   42

Mama tucked the package into her bag. "Ai-Yi-Yi! You and I will be   55

lucky to share half a pancake."   61

"But Mama, we have a little bit and a little bit more."   73

Intonation

B	☐ Does not change pitch.	A	☐ Changes pitch to match some of the content.
I	☐ Changes pitch, but does not match content.	AH	☐ Changes pitch to match all of the content.

Accuracy and Rate Formula

Use the formula to measure a reader's accuracy and rate while reading aloud.

_____   –   _____   =   _____

| words attempted in one minute | number of errors | words corrected per minute (wcpm) |

Reading Options: Double-Entry Log

Ba's Business

Fill in details from the story as you read "Ba's Business."

Page	What I read	What it means to me

Tell a partner what you would have done to sell more egg tarts.

Name _____ Date _____

Compare Characters

Compare the characters from the two stories.

	Beginning of Story	End of Story	Why does the character change?
Mama Panya	She is worried about having enough food.		
Ba			

 Talk with a partner about which story you liked better and why.

4.9

Name _____   Date _____

Grammar: Present Tense

Farmer's Market

Grammar Rules Present-Tense Action Verbs

A present-tense action verb must agree with its subject.

Use **-s** at the end of an action verb if the subject is **he**, **she**, or **it**.	Carmella **loves** street fairs. She **takes** me along with her.
Do **not** add -s to the verb if the subject is **I**, **you**, **we**, or **they**.	Buyers **walk** slowly through the fairs. They **buy** a lot of things.

Fill in each blank with the present-tense verb form that agrees with the subject.

My parents _____ us to the farmer's market. We _____
(take)   (enjoy)

all the sights, smells, and sounds. Farmers _____ vegetables
(sell)

and fruit. One farmer _____ flowers, too. My mother _____
(sell)   (buy)

flowers every week. She _____ flowers. One man _____
(love)   (cook)

delicious burritos. A woman _____ faces. Two men _____
(paint)   (carve)

wooden toys. They _____ out to buyers. The farmer's market is
(call)

so much fun! It _____ me smile.
(make)

 Choose three verbs from the story and write new sentences. Read them to a partner.

© National Geographic Learning, a part of Cengage Learning, Inc.

Name _____   Date _____

What Do You Think?

Make an opinion chart of your partner's opinion.

Opinion:

Evidence:

Evidence:

Evidence:

 Ask your partner questions about his or her opinion.

Grammar: Helping Verbs

Let's Go to the Play!

Grammar Rules Helping Verbs: *can, could, should*

A helping verb tells more about the main verb.

- *Can* shows what someone is able to do: *I **can** run fast.*
- *Could* shows a choice or possible action: *I **could** win a race.*
- *Should* shows an opinion: *I **should** practice more first.*

Choose the correct helping verb to complete each sentence. Use the clue at the end of each sentence to help you.

1. Greta ___*should*___ go to the play. (opinion)
   (could/should)

2. You _____ see the play, too. (opinion)
   (should/can)

3. Roberto _____ go with you. (able to)
   (can/should)

4. I _____ go, but I'd rather see a movie. (possible action)
   (can/could)

5. We _____ go to the play next week, though. (choice)
   (could/can)

 Talk to a partner about things the two of you can do, could do, and should do after school.

Name _____ Date _____

A Better Way

Every year, the Earth loses many trees. They are cut down to make room for farming. This is called "slash-and-burn agriculture." People also want to use the trees for wood. The forests are disappearing!

Paola Segura and Cid Simões think there is a better way. They want to save trees and help people. They teach farmers how to use the same, small piece of land many times.

Farmers live on the land and make money by growing plants. They do not use "slash-and-burn agriculture."

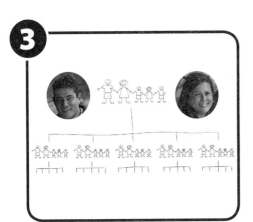

To make a difference, many farmers need to grow plants this way. Segura and Simões teach one family what to do. That family teaches five other families. Each family will teach five other families.

Segura and Simões call this the 5 x 5 system. Many trees will be saved. Families will live better lives because of sustainable farming.

© National Geographic Learning, a part of Cengage Learning, Inc.

Grammar: Helping Verbs

Helping Verb Tic-Tac-Toe

Grammar Rules Helping Verbs: *may, must, have to, has to*

Use *may* to show permission or possibility: *I **may** be late today.*

Use *must, has to,* or *have to* to show what someone needs to do:
> *I **must** go to the doctor after school.*
> *I **have to** go to the doctor after school.*
> *My mother **has to** take me.*

Choose a box. To draw an **X** in a box, player A makes a *may* statement. To draw an **O** in a box, player B makes a *must* statement. The first player to get three **X**s or **O**s in a row wins. Switch roles and play again. This time, player B makes statements with *has to* or *have to*.

 Tell your partner a way to work together on a classroom task. Use *may* and *must*.

Vocabulary: Apply Word Knowledge

Vocabulary Bingo

1. Write one Key Word in each tree.

2. Listen to the clues. Find the Key Word and use a marker to cover it.

3. Say "Bingo!" when you have four markers in a row or column.

● **Reread and Explain: Opinion Chart**

A Better Way

Make an opinion chart for pages 254–257 in "A Better Way."

Opinion: Sustainable agriculture is good for the farmer and good for the land.

Evidence: It lets farmers grow crops on the same land year after year.
Evidence:
Evidence:

💬 **Explain the opinion and evidence to a partner.**

© National Geographic Learning, a part of Cengage Learning, Inc.

Fluency: Phrasing

A Better Way

Use this passage to practice reading with proper phrasing.

To make a difference, many farmers need to grow crops this way.	12
Segura and Simões use a special plan to teach more farmers. It is	25
called the 5 x 5 System. First, they teach one family how to grow	39
crops that don't ruin the land. Then that family teaches five new	51
families what they learned. Each new family teaches five more	61
families. Think of all the land that could be saved in the future!	74

Phrasing

B ☐ Rarely pauses while reading the text.   A ☐ Frequently pauses at appropriate points in the text.

I ☐ Occasionally pauses while reading the text.   AH ☐ Consistently pauses at all appropriate points in the text.

Accuracy and Rate Formula

Use the formula below to measure a reader's accuracy and rate while reading aloud.

$$\underline{\hspace{3cm}} - \underline{\hspace{3cm}} = \underline{\hspace{3cm}}$$

words attempted   number of errors   words correct per minute
in one minute   (wcpm)

Name _____   Date _____

The Ant and the Grasshopper

Complete these forms as you read "The Ant and the Grasshopper."

Word Detective

New Word: _____

What I think it means: _____

_____

🔍 Clues: _____

📖 Definition: _____

_____

- ✂

Word Detective

New Word: _____

What I think it means: _____

_____

🔍 Clues: _____

_____

📖 Definition: _____

_____

💬 **Use one of your new words in a sentence about the grasshopper or the ant. Tell a partner. Then tell how you might use the word again.**

Compare Purposes

Compare authors' purposes in "A Better Way" and "The Ant and the Grasshopper."

Title	Topic	Author's Purpose
"A Better Way" by Juan Quintana	sustainable agriculture	
"The Ant and the Grasshopper" by Shirleyann Costigan		

Take turns with a partner telling how the authors' purposes are alike or different.

Grammar: *be/have*; Subject-Verb Agreement

What Is in the Garden?

Grammar Rules *be/have*; Subject-Verb Agreement

The verbs *be* and *have* are irregular. The subject and verb must agree. Use these correct forms:

I am	We are	I have	We have
You are	You are	You have	You have
He, she, it is	They are	He, she, it has	They have

Write the correct form of *be* or *have* to complete each sentence. Choose the correct form for the subject.

Jenna and Jake ___*have*___ a large garden. Jake's favorite vegetable _____ corn. He _____ several rows of corn in the garden. The corn _____ almost ready to harvest. Both Jenna and Jake _____ excited to roast ears of corn. They also grow tomatoes. Tomatoes _____ their mother's favorite vegetable. Jenna planted sunflowers, too. They _____ delicious seeds and pretty blooms.

   I _____ planning to help them pick some corn. I _____ a basket I will take with me.

 Imagine a garden. Tell your partner about it, using forms of *be* and *have*.

Ideas

Every writer has a special way of saying things, or a voice. The voice should sound genuine, or real, and be unique to that writer.

	Is the message clear and interesting?	Do the details show the writer knows the topic?
4	❏ All of the writing is clear and focused. ❏ The writing is very interesting.	❏ All the details tell about the topic. The writer knows the topic well.
3	❏ Most of the writing is clear and focused. ❏ Most of the writing is interesting.	❏ Most of the details are about the topic. The writer knows the topic fairly well.
2	❏ Some of the writing is not clear. The writing lacks some focus. ❏ Some of the writing is confusing.	❏ Some details are about the topic. The writer doesn't know the topic well.
1	❏ The writing is not clear or focused. ❏ The writing is confusing.	❏ Many details are not about the topic. The writer does not know the topic.

Name _____   Date _____

Writing Project: Prewrite

Opinion Chart

Complete the opinion chart for your persuasive essay.

Opinion:
Evidence:
Evidence:
Evidence:
Evidence:
Evidence:
Evidence:

© National Geographic Learning, a part of Cengage Learning, Inc.

For use with TE p. T269b   **4.22**   Unit 4 | Let's Work Together

Writing Project

Revise

Use the Revising Marks to revise this paragraph. Look for:

- a clear opinion
- supporting ideas
- persuasive language

Revising Marks	
∧	Add.
ℐ	Take out.
⌒⌐	Move to here.

We could take meals to people who are housebound. These are people who cannot for some reason leave their homes.

Getting meals would make them feel less lonely. They would also eat good meals.

We will feel better if we do this.

Writing Project

Edit and Proofread

Use the Editing Marks to edit and proofread this paragraph. Look for:

- **verbs**
- **subject-verb agreement**
- **comma after an introductory phrase**

Editing Marks	
∧	Add.
℘	Take out.
⟲	Move to here.
◯	Check spelling.
⌄	Add comma.

I think that the best thing that our community did was to start

a lunch program for the homeless. At the community center every

Saturday my friends and I serves lunch to twelve guests. Once a

month we also prepare a dinner. It is a good feeling to be able to

help others.

Name _____   Date _____

Mysteries of Matter

Make a concept map with the answers to the Big Question: What causes matter to change?

What causes matter to change?

Thinking Map: Character-Plot Chart

Partner Skit

Make a character-plot chart about your skit.

Character	What the Character Says	What This Shows About the Character	What This Shows About the Plot

 Take turns telling a partner about one of the characters. What do the character's words show about the character?

Grammar: Adjectives

What's It Like?

Grammar Rules Adjectives

An adjective describes a noun.

An adjective can describe how something looks, smells, tastes, feels, or sounds.

An adjective can also tell how many or what things are made of.

An adjective usually comes before the noun it describes.

Write an adjective in each blank.

| tiny | three | wet | strawberry | warm | bright |

1. The _____ sunshine wakes me up.

2. The _____ snow begins to melt.

3. The _____ grass starts to grow.

4. I pour _____ jam on _____ pancakes.

5. I am ready for a _____ day.

 Use three adjectives to tell a partner about something you saw or did today.

Key Points Reading

Melt the Snow!

It was a long winter. Now Hormiguita wants to go outside and play. The sun is shining and the snow is melting.

Mami says Hormiguita can go, but to be careful. The air is cold. It could start snowing again. Hormiguita tells Mami not to worry. She goes out to play.

Hormiguita is playing in the forest. Suddenly, the Wind blows and a Cloud moves in front of the Sun. It starts to snow. Hormiguita wants to go home, but her leg is trapped in the Snow!

Hormiguita asks the Snow, the Sun, the Cloud, the Wind, and the Wall to help her. They are not strong enough, but the Mouse is. He frees Hormiguita.

Hormiguita hugs the Mouse and says "thank you." She runs home to Mami. Hormiguita is happy to be home.

Grammar: Adjectives

The Comparing Game

Grammar Rules Adjectives That Compare

To compare two persons, places, or things, add **-er** to most adjectives. For some long adjectives, use the word **more**.

cold**er**   bright**er**   **more** powerful

To compare three or more persons, places, or things, add **-est**, or use the word **most**.

cold**est**   bright**est**   **most** powerful

Some adjectives show how much or how many: **few, many**

1. **Play with a partner.**
2. **Toss a coin. Heads moves one space. Tails moves two spaces.**
3. **Say a sentence using the correct adjective.**

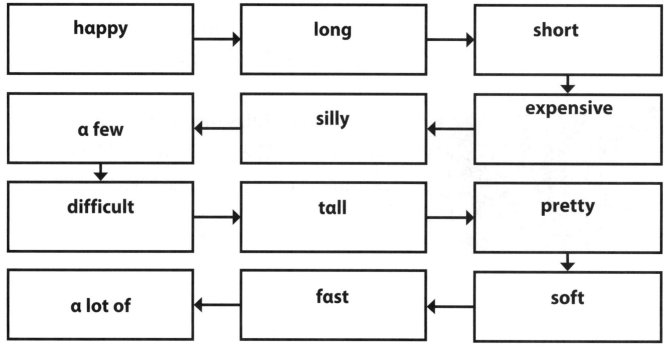

happy	→	long	→	short

a few	←	silly	←	expensive

difficult	→	tall	→	pretty

a lot of	←	fast	←	soft

5.5

Reread and Explain: Character-Plot Chart

Melt the Snow!

Make a character-plot chart of "Melt the Snow!"

Character	What the Character Says	What This Shows About the Character	What This Shows About the Plot
Mami	"Don't go far, and be very careful."	Mami wants Hormiguita to be safe.	Mami lets Hormiguita go out to play.
Hormiguita			

 How does the play's dialogue help you understand its characters and plot? Use your character-plot chart to explain this to a partner.

Name _____ Date _____

Melt the Snow!

Use this passage to practice reading with proper expression.

Hormiguita: (pointing): ¡Mami, *mira*! Look,   3

the sun is shining. It's melting the snow.   11

It's been such a long winter, and I'm tired of   21

staying indoors. May I go out and play?   29

Fluency: Expression

[B] ☐ Does not read with feeling.   [A] ☐ Reads with appropriate feeling for most content.

[I] ☐ Reads with some feeling, but does not match content.   [AH] ☐ Reads with appropriate feeling for all content.

Accuracy and Rate Formula

Use the formula to measure a reader's accuracy and rate while reading aloud.

_____ − _____ = _____
words attempted in one minute   number of errors   words correct per minute (wcpm)

Name _____ Date _____

Saved in Ice

Complete these fact cards as you read "Saved in Ice."

- ✂ - -

That's Amazing!

An amazing fact about _____

is _____

_____

I found it in the article _____

by _____

_____   _____

Name   Date

- ✂ - -

That's Amazing!

An amazing fact about _____

is _____

_____

I found it in the article _____

by _____

_____   _____

Name   Date

- ✂ - -

_____

Name _____ Date _____

Compare Media

Compare an e-mail and a Web-based article.

	Rudy's e-mail	"Saved in Ice"
electronic communication	yes	yes
formal language		
informal language		
personal information		
factual information		

 Talk with a partner. Tell whether you liked the article and why.

Grammar: Adjectives and Articles

The Storm

Grammar Rules Adjectives and Articles

Some adjectives tell "which one."

This day is warm. Was it warm **that** day?

These clouds are big. Were **those** clouds bigger?

Articles identify nouns.

An animal died in Russia. **The** mammoth was about as big as **a** dog.

Write an adjective or an article in each blank.

_____ storm is starting today. _____ storm reminds me of one last year. In _____ storm _____ inch of rain fell every hour. Then _____ rain turned into snow. Winds knocked down _____ tree, too. I hope today's storm is smaller. I hope _____ winds are softer. I like _____ tree I can see here. I want to climb _____ tree after the storm.

💬 **Use three adjectives and articles to tell a partner a weather story.**

Why Did It Happen?

Make a cause-and-effect chart about something that happened.

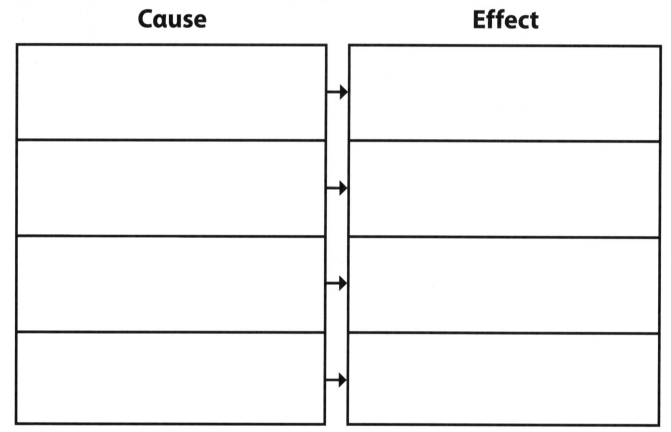

Cause	Effect

Talk with a partner about a game. Tell what happened to cause another event to happen.

Grammar: Possessive Adjectives

Day at the Pond

Grammar Rules Possessive Adjectives

A possessive adjective tells who or what owns, has, or is part of something. Put the possessive adjective before the noun.

One	More Than One
my	our
your	your
his, her, its	their

Read the first sentence in each pair. Then write a possessive adjective in the second sentence so that it has the same meaning.

1. Today, I walk to the beach with <u>the friends that I have.</u>

   Today, I walk to the beach with _____ friends

2. "Wear <u>the mittens that you own,</u>" said Ana.

   "Wear _____ mittens," said Ana.

3. There is hot chocolate in <u>the backpack that we have.</u>

   There is hot chocolate in _____ backpack.

4. They were glad they wore <u>the boots they own.</u>

   They were glad they wore _____ boots.

 Use two possessive adjectives from the chart. Tell your partner about something you and a friend own, have, or are part of.

Key Points Reading

Quicksand!

Some people are afraid of quicksand. Movies show people drowning in it. You can find quicksand in places where there is a lot of water. Quicksand is not really dangerous. It is just sand and water. There is so much water in the sand that it cannot hold anything up.

Most of the time, the ground is strong. It can hold a person, a car, or a building.

When there is too much water, it pushes the very small sand or dirt pieces away from each other. Then the ground is not strong anymore.

Some people believe scary things about quicksand. They think it is alive or that worms that suck blood are in it. These things are not true. Next time you see quicksand in a movie, don't be scared!

Grammar: Possessive Nouns

The Possessives Game

Grammar Rules Possessive Nouns

A possessive noun tells who or what owns or has something.

For a singular noun, add *'s*: the cat's tail, Rita's books, a dog's paw

For a plural noun, add *s'*: kids' sneakers, cars' lights, lions' roars

1. **Play with a partner.**

2. **Cut out the cards. Turn the cards face down.**

3. **Choose one bigger card and one smaller card. If they form the correct possessive noun, keep them. If not, put them face down again.**

one lion __ teeth	the sand __ temperature	two bear __ claws	a fish __ scales
a few bird __ feathers	five team __ uniforms	ten duck __ quacks	a camel __ hump
ten flower __ seeds	the water __ weight	a school __ students	a room __ shape

's	's	s'	's
s'	s'	s'	's
s'	's	's	's

Name _____ Date _____

Quicksand: When Earth Turns to Liquid

Cause		Effect
Water sinks into the sand.	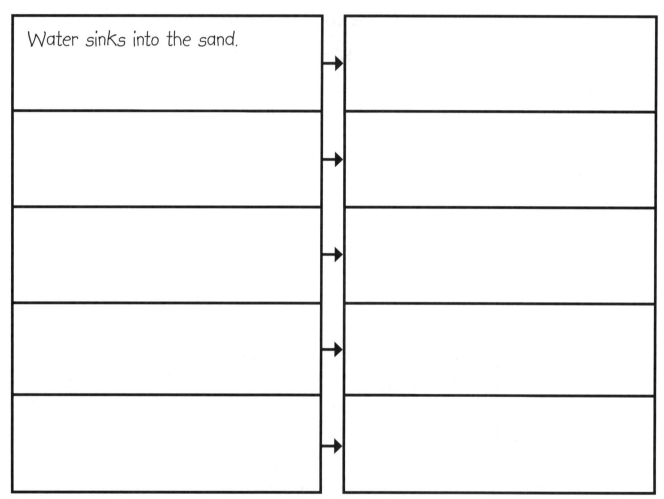	

 Use your cause-and-effect chart to summarize the selection for a partner.

Fluency: Intonation

Quicksand: When Earth Turns to Liquid

Use this passage to practice reading with proper intonation.

What Is Quicksand?

The word *quicksand* makes some people shiver with fear.	9
This is probably because of the way many movies show	19
quicksand. In films, quicksand is often a mysterious substance	28
that sucks people and animals to their deaths!	36
Actual quicksand is very different from movie quicksand.	44
It rarely harms people or animals. Real quicksand is not	54
mysterious. It is a simple substance that forms naturally.	63

Fluency: Intonation

B ☐ Does not change pitch.   A ☐ Changes pitch to match some of the content.

I ☐ Changes pitch, but does not match content.   AH ☐ Changes pitch to match all of the content.

Accuracy and Rate Formula

Use the formula to measure a reader's accuracy and rate while reading aloud.

$$\underline{\hspace{3cm}} - \underline{\hspace{3cm}} = \underline{\hspace{3cm}}$$

words attempted   number of errors   words correct per minute
in one minute   (wcpm)

Name _____ Date _____

Meet Maycira Costa

Complete this chart as you read "Meet Maycira Costa."

Page	What I read	What it means to me

 Tell a partner what part of the selection was most interesting and why.

Respond and Extend: Venn Diagram

Compare Text Features

Compare a science article and an interview.

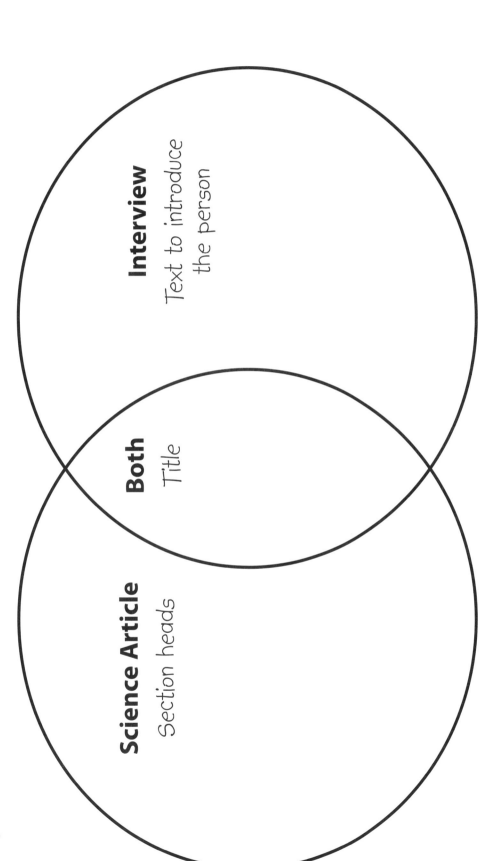

Interview

Text to introduce the person

Both

Title

Science Article

Section heads

Take turns with a partner. Interview each other about the science article and the interview. What text features did you like?

Grammar: Possessive Nouns and Adjectives

Creatures of the Wetlands

Grammar Rules Possessive Nouns and Adjectives

	One Owner	More Than One Owner
Possessive Nouns: Use an apostrophe and an *s*.	an alligator's teeth	the crabs' claws
Possessive Adjectives: Use the correct word for one or more owners.	my, your, his, her, its	our, your, their

Write the correct form of the possessive noun or adjective.

_____Nita's_____ family visited a wetland. They rode in two _____
(Nita's/Nitas')   (guide's/guides')

boats. Her two _____ hands tickled the _____
(brother's/brothers')   (water's/waters')

surface. They pulled _____ hands back when they heard a splash.
(his/their)

The guide said a _____ favorite tree is the
(mudskipper's/mudskippers')

mangrove. _____ fish story is true! Mudskippers are fish
(Her/Our)

that climb _____ branches.
(mangrove's/mangroves')

 Use a possessive noun to write a new title for the story. Read your title to a partner. Check to see if your partner used an apostrophe and an *s* correctly.

© National Geographic Learning, a part of Cengage Learning, Inc.

Name _____ Date _____

Ideas

Every writer has a special way of saying things, or a voice. The voice should sound genuine, or real, and be unique to that writer.

	Is the message clear and interesting?	Do the details show the writer knows the topic?
4	❑ All of the writing is clear and focused. ❑ The writing is very interesting.	❑ All the details tell about the topic. The writer knows the topic well.
3	❑ Most of the writing is clear and focused. ❑ Most of the writing is interesting.	❑ Most of the details are about the topic. The writer knows the topic fairly well.
2	❑ Some of the writing is not clear. The writing lacks some focus. ❑ Some of the writing is confusing.	❑ Some details are about the topic. The writer doesn't know the topic well.
1	❑ The writing is not clear or focused. ❑ The writing is confusing.	❑ Many details are not about the topic. The writer does not know the topic.

Name _____   Date _____

Cause-and-Effect Chart

Complete the cause-and-effect chart for your literary response.

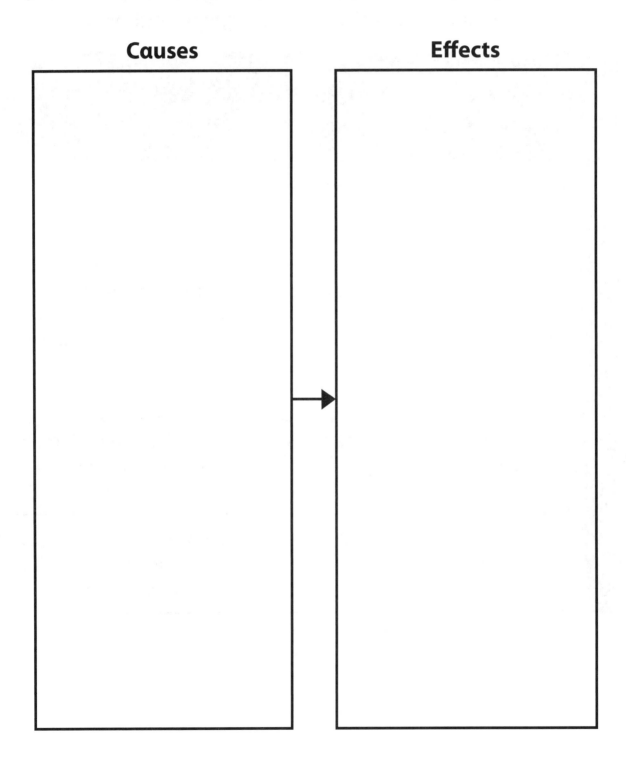

Causes	**Effects**

5.21

Name _____ Date _____

Revise

Use the Revising Marks to revise this literary response paragraph. Look for:

- clear opinions
- details that support the opinions

Revising Marks	
∧	Add.
℘	Take out.
⌒‿∧	Move to here.

"Quicksand: When Earth Turns to Liquid" is a science article that

gives facts about quicksand. There are lots of photos, too. I like it

because I learned things. Finally, there was another thing I liked.

Writing Project

Edit and Proofread

Use the Editing Marks to edit and proofread this paragraph. Look for:

- **correct spelling with** *-ed* **and** *-ing*
- **correct use of apostrophes with possessive nouns**
- **correct possessive adjectives**

Editing Marks	
∧	Add.
℘	Take out.
⌄	Add apostrophe.

I thought that "Melt the Snow!" was a very funny play. I laughed when I read that a snowflake was traping Hormiguitas leg. It was funny to think that Cloud, Wind, and Wall were all stoping Sun from shining, but little Mouses chewing helped them all. "Melt the Snow!" is one of her favorite stories. I hope my sister reads it in their class, too.

Name _____   Date _____

From Past to Present

Make a concept map with the answers to the Big Question: How can we preserve our traditions?

How can we preserve our traditions?

Thinking Map: Details Web

At the Festival

Make a details web about things at the festival.

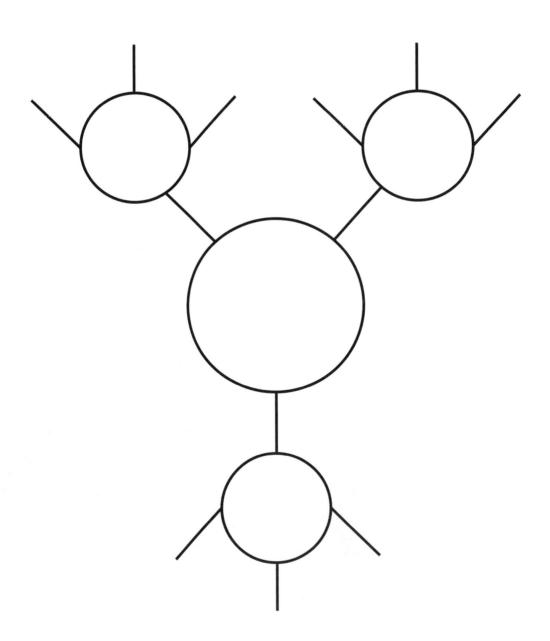

Grammar: Subject Pronouns

Fun at the Fair

Grammar Rules Subject Pronouns

A pronoun takes the place of a noun. A subject pronoun is the subject of the sentence.

Subject Pronouns	
Use for One	**Use for More Than One**
I	we
you	you
he, she, it	they

Fill in the blanks with subject pronouns.

Dear Carmela,

   Last Saturday, my family went to the fair. _____ all had a great time. My sister loves rides. _____ rode the roller coaster. _____ looked too scary for me. I played games instead. My father loves salsa music. _____ danced with my mother. _____ were very good! What did I do? _____ ate a taco. _____ was delicious! _____ should come with us next time!

Your friend,
Alma

 Tell a partner about something you did with your family or friends. Use subject pronouns.

Oye, Celia!

1 A girl listens to Celia Cruz singing. She hears and feels many things as she listens to the music.

She hears the *stroom stroom* of the guitar and the *doong doong* of the drums.

She thinks of Cuba. It is the country she and Celia Cruz are both from.

2 The girl hears Celia sing about Cuba with sadness and love.

She wants to cry because she misses Cuba. But she feels happy, too.

3 The girl hears her history in the music. She hears herself in Celia's songs. She loves to dance when she hears Celia's music. It makes her happy. Celia's music makes everyone happy.

Name _____ Date _____

Winning with Pronouns

Grammar Rules Object Pronouns

Use object pronouns in the predicate of a sentence. The object pronouns are *me, you, him, her, it, us, you,* and *them.*

1. Play with a partner. Place your markers on *music.*
2. Toss a coin. Move one space for heads. Move two spaces for tails.
3. If you land on an object pronoun, say it in a sentence.

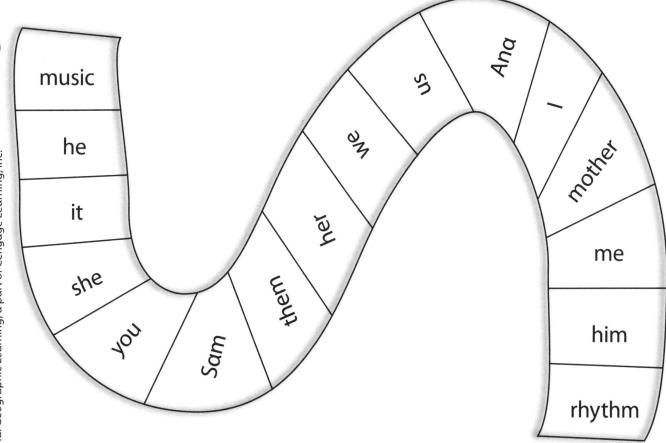

Tell a partner about something you saw or watched. Use object pronouns.

Name _____   Date _____

Oye, Celia!

Make a details web about Celia Cruz's music.

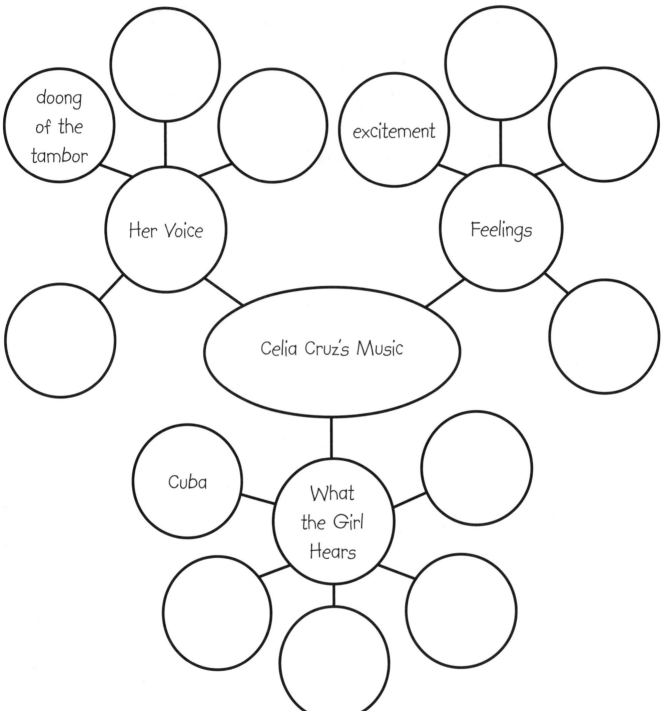

Use your details web to describe your favorite parts of the song to a partner.

Oye, Celia!

Use this passage to practice reading with proper expression.

Unforgettable Celia,	2
When I hear you, I hear *la historia*—	10
Your history, my history,	14
Our history.	16
Your lyrics breathe life into our ancestors—	23
Slaves who gathered in stolen moments	29
To create a rhythm	33
That was passed down to us.	39
I thank them.	42

Expression

B ☐ Does not read with feeling

I ☐ Reads with some feeling, but does not match content.

A ☐ Reads with appropriate feeling for most content.

AH ☐ Reads with appropriate feeling for all content.

Accuracy and Rate Formula

Use the formula below to measure a reader's accuracy and rate while reading aloud.

$$\underline{\hspace{3cm}} - \underline{\hspace{3cm}} = \underline{\hspace{3cm}}$$

words attempted in one minute	number of errors	words correct per minute (wcpm)

Name _____   Date _____

Blues Legend: Blind Lemon Jefferson

Complete this journal as you read "Blues Legend: Blind Lemon Jefferson."

What I think	What do you think?
Pages: _____ _____ _____ _____	_____ _____ _____ _____
Pages: _____ _____ _____ _____	_____ _____ _____ _____
Pages: _____ _____ _____ _____	_____ _____ _____ _____

 Tell a partner what you thought about Blind Lemon Jefferson.

© National Geographic Learning, a part of Cengage Learning, Inc.

Name _____ Date _____

Compare Language

Compare the language used in the lyrics to the language in the biography.

Sensory Language in the Lyrics	Facts in the Biography
1. Her voice is like the doong-doong-doong of the tambor.	1. Jefferson was born in Texas.
2.	2.
3.	3.
4.	4.

 Talk with a partner about the kind of language you hear in a favorite song. Then compare that language with the language in the biography.

Grammar: Pronoun Agreement

My Musical Family

Grammar Rules Pronoun Agreement

	One	More than One
Use **subject** pronouns in the subject of a sentence.	I, you, he, she, it	we, you, they
Use **object** pronouns in the predicate of a sentence.	me, you, him, her, it	us, you, them

What pronouns can take the place of the underlined nouns? Write the correct subject or object pronoun on the line.

1. My brother and I like music. <u>My brother and I</u> play instruments. _____

2. I play the trumpet. I have played <u>the trumpet</u> since I was six years old. _____

3. My sister plays the guitar. <u>My sister</u> strums it and sings. _____

4. My father plays the piano. Many people ask <u>my father</u> for lessons. _____

5. My grandmother is a good singer. People often invite <u>my grandmother</u> to sing. _____

 Tell a partner about people in your family and the music they like. Use subject and object pronouns correctly.

Name _____   Date _____

Thinking Map: Flow Chart

Steps in a Process

Make a flow chart to show the steps of how to make something.

This is how to make a _____ .

Flow Chart

Step 1:

⬇

Step 2:

⬇

Step 3:

⬇

Step 4:

Name _____   Date _____

3rl

Near _____ _____ ay?

Gramm _____ **uns**

A demo _____ things near you
or far aw _____

Demonstrative Pronouns		
	One	**More Than One**
Near You	this	these
Far Away	that	those

A. **Read the two sentences. Then write _this, that, these,_ or _those_ to complete the second sentence.**

1. Here is a music book. Give _____ to Mr. Lopez.

2. The drums are across the room. Take _____ to the music room.

3. Get the poster boards from the closet. _____ will work best for your poster.

4. Here are some good markers. _____ are bright colors.

5. We will use the bulletin board in the hall. _____ will be a good place for the poster.

B. **Draw yourself at the center of a picture. Draw things near you and far away. Then label the things _this, that, these,_ or _those._**

_____ **Tell a partner how you labeled each object in your picture.**

Carving Stories in Cedar: How to Make a Totem Pole

1

Hundreds of years ago, the first people who lived on the northwest coast of Canada and the United States wanted to tell stories about the past. They were not able to write their stories, so they made totem poles.

Totem poles are family stories. Sometimes they are called silent books.

Israel Shotridge has carved totem poles for 20 years. Here are the steps he takes to make a totem pole:

2

a.    d.

b.    e.

c.    f.

a. He chooses a design.

b. He gets the tree ready. He draws pictures on the wood.

c. He carves the pole with special tools.

d. He paints the pole traditional colors like red, green, blue, and black.

e. When the totem pole is finished, everyone works together to raise it.

f. The pole is finished. It is time for a big party!

Grammar: Possessive Pronouns

Whose Project Is It?

Grammar Rules Possessive Pronouns

A possessive pronoun tells who or what owns something.

Possessive Pronouns	
One Owner	**More Than One Owner**
mine	ours
yours	yours
his, hers, its	theirs

Write the correct possessive pronoun.

1. Your class will visit ____ours____ to see our projects.
   (ours, theirs)

2. Ben is still working on _____ .
   (mine, his)

3. Lynn has finished _____ . She made a clay pot.
   (hers, yours)

4. Maya made a quilt. "Can I see _____?" she asked me.
   (yours, ours)

5. "I just finished _____," I said. I held up my painting.
   (theirs, mine)

Use two possessive pronouns. Tell about something you have and something your partner has.

Vocabulary Bingo

1. Write one Key Word in each mask.

2. Listen to the clues. Find the Key Word and use a marker to cover it.

3. Say "Bingo!" when you have four markers in a row.

How Shotridge Makes a Totem Pole

Make a flow chart of "How Shotridge Makes a Totem Pole."

Flow Chart

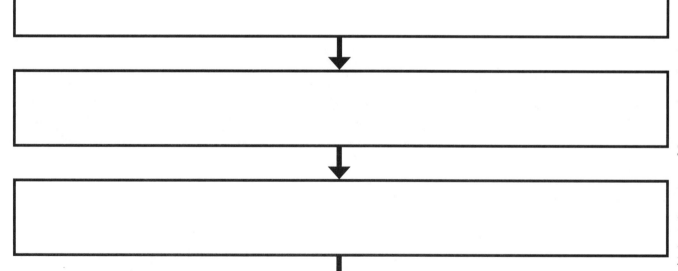

1. Shotridge chooses a design.

2. He prepares the tree. He removes the bark and draws the design.

 Use your flow chart to explain the steps to a partner.

Name _____ Date _____

© National Geographic Learning, a part of Cengage Learning, Inc.

Fluency: Intonation

The Legend of Raven and Fog Woman

Use this passage to practice reading with proper intonation.

Raven asked, "How did you do that?"	7
Fog Woman didn't answer.	11
Day after day she filled the basket with water, and	21
soon the creek ran bright with salmon. No one in the	32
village went hungry.	35
But Raven wasn't satisfied. He clawed the ground with	44
his feet and flapped his wings angrily.	51
"Tell me your secret," Raven demanded.	57
Fog Woman wouldn't answer.	61
Raven lost his temper. "If you won't tell me, then go!"	72
he shouted.	74

Intonation

B ☐ Does not change pitch.   A ☐ Changes pitch to match some of the content.

I ☐ Changes pitch, but does not match content.   AH ☐ Changes pitch to match all of the content.

Accuracy and Rate Formula

Use the formula below to measure a reader's intonation while reading aloud.

$$\underset{\substack{\text{Words attempted} \\ \text{in one minute}}}{\rule{3cm}{0.4pt}} - \underset{\text{number of errors}}{\rule{3cm}{0.4pt}} = \underset{\substack{\text{words correct per minute} \\ \text{(wcpm)}}}{\rule{3cm}{0.4pt}}$$

Read the Profile and Folk Tale

Complete one Strategy Planner for "Stories to Tell" and another for "The Rainbow Bridge."

Title:			

1. What is the author's purpose for writing?

	to tell a story		to give information
	to entertain		

2. What is your purpose for reading?

	for enjoyment		to get information

3. What type of selection are you going to read?

	fiction		nonfiction

Do the following:	**Do the following:**
• Identify the characters and setting. • Think about what happens and when it happens.	• Read more slowly. • Identify facts about real people or events. • Use text features to find more information.

 How did the strategies help you understand the selections? Tell a partner which strategy was most helpful to you.

Name _____   Date _____

Compare Themes

Compare the legend and folk tale themes.

Title: "The Legend of Raven and Fog Woman"

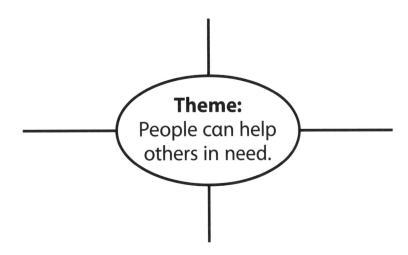

Theme:
People can help
others in need.

Title: "The Rainbow Bridge"

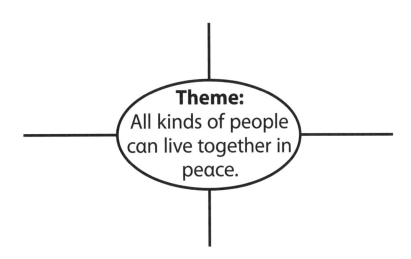

Theme:
All kinds of people
can live together in
peace.

Take turns with a partner. Use the Theme Webs to talk about how
the themes of the two tales are alike and different.

Grammar: Pronoun Agreement

The Possessive Pronoun Game

Grammar Rules Pronoun Agreement

Possessive pronouns tell who or what owns something.
Be sure to use the right possessive pronoun.

- For yourself, use **mine**
- For yourself and one or more people, use **ours**.
- When you speak to one or more people, use **yours**.
- For one other person or thing, use **his**, **hers**, or **its**.
- For two or more people or things, use **theirs**.

1. **Play with a partner.**
2. **Spin the spinner.**
3. **Say a sentence using the possessive pronoun.**

Make a Spinner

1. Push a brad 🔩 through the center of the spinner.

2. Open the brad on the back.

3. Hook a paper clip ▭ over the brad on the front to make a spinner.

Name _____ Date _____

Organization

Writing is organized when it is easy to follow. All the ideas make sense together and flow from one idea to the next in an order that fits the writer's audience and purpose.

	Is the writing organized? Does it fit the audience and purpose?	Does the writing flow?
4	❑ The writing is very well-organized. ❑ It clearly fits both the writer's audience and purpose.	❑ The writing is smooth and logical. Each sentence flows into the next one.
3	❑ Most of the writing is organized. ❑ It mostly fits the writer's audience and purpose.	❑ Most of the writing is smooth. There are only a few sentences that do not flow logically.
2	❑ The writing is not well-organized. ❑ It fits the writer's audience or the writer's purpose, but not both.	❑ Some of the writing is smooth. Many sentences do not flow smoothly.
1	❑ The writing is not organized at all. ❑ It does not fit the writer's audience or purpose.	❑ The sentences do not flow smoothly or logically.

Details Web

Complete the details web for your interview.

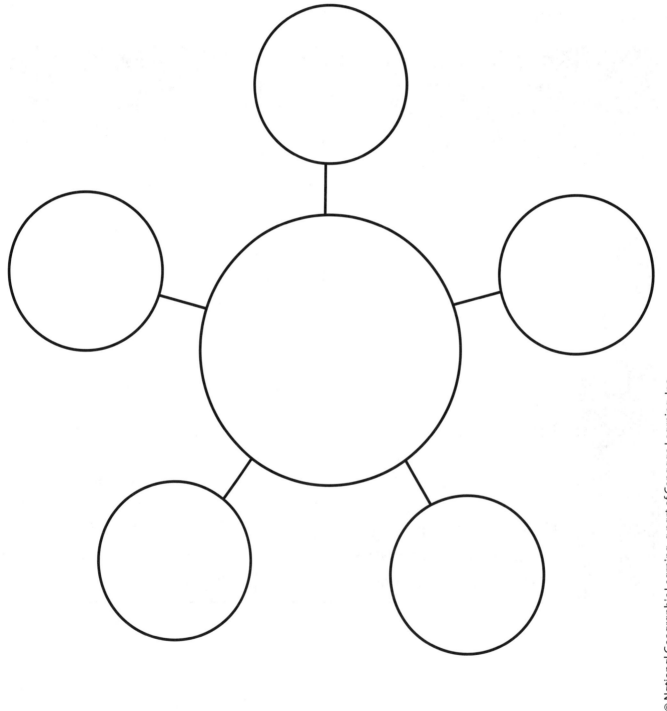

© National Geographic Learning, a part of Cengage Learning, Inc.

Name ______________________ Date ______________

Writing Project

Revise

Use the Revising Marks to revise this interview. Look for:

- precise words
- strong beginning and ending
- logical order of questions

Revising Marks	
^	Add.
℘	Take out.
⊂⊃⌒	Move to here.

Patchwork quilts are a special tradition of the American people. Many of them look nice.

Nadia: Why do you think it's important to preserve this tradition?

Aunt Paula: Because it's a reminder of the pioneers who settled parts of America a long time ago. It's a part of our history.

Nadia: What are patchwork quilts?

Aunt Paula: Patchwork is a type of quilt made with small pieces of fabric. Pioneer women had to make do with what they had, so they used small scraps of clothing and fabric to patch together a quilt.

Name _____   Date _____

Edit and Proofread

Use the Editing Marks to edit and proofread this paragraph. Look for:
- pronouns
- correct spelling of homophones
- capitalization of names and holidays

Editing Marks	
∧	Add.
ℐ	Take out.
⬯↵	Move to here.
⬯	Check spelling.
≡	Capitalize.

Me interviewed my cousin maria about how to make a piñata four

birthday celebrations, christmas, and other holidays. Her makes

beautiful paintings on boxes. Then, she fills them with candies. She

wraps them in colorful foil paper and hangs them from a tree or a

place on the wall. They are saw pretty. my brothers and me don't

want to knock them down at first to get the candy! But, then we

finally do!

Unit Concept Map

Blast! Crash! Splash!

Make a concept map with the answers to the Big Question: What forces can change Earth?

What forces can change Earth?

Name _____ Date _____

Title: _____

Make an imagery chart about your story.

Place	Person	Thing

Use imagery to tell your partner another story.

Name _____   Date _____

The Storm

Grammar Rules Adverbs

An adverb describes a verb. It tells where, when, or how.

Tell where	Tell when	Tell how
I looked **down**.	It is raining **now**.	I ran **quickly**.

Circle each adverb. Decide if it tells where, when, or how. Write each adverb in the correct place on the chart.

The wind blew hard yesterday. I looked up. Dark clouds rushed above. Rain started to fall lightly. Then, I heard a crash of thunder. The rain poured everywhere! I ran fast. I got to my house soon.

where	when	how
up		
_____	_____	_____
_____	_____	_____

💬 **Tell a partner about a storm you saw. Use adverbs.**

Name _____ Date _____

An Island Grows

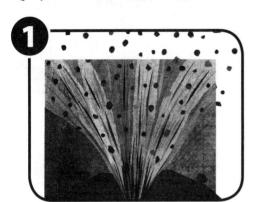

1 Deep under the ocean, rocks break apart. Water moves. A volcano blows lava into the water.

Rocks come up from the ocean. The waves hit the rocks and sand piles up. An island is growing in the ocean. Trees and plants grow on the new island. Birds come to the island to live. Bugs live here, too.

2 Then, people see the island. Sailors use maps to find it. Settlers stay on the island. They build houses and use the soil to grow food. They have markets where people can buy and sell fish, fruit, and vegetables.

3 The island is busy with people and animals. But one day, near the island, the water moves. A volcano blows lava into the water. Another island is growing!

Grammar: Adverbs

Build a Story

Grammar Rules Adverbs

To compare two actions, add *-er* to an adverb, or use the words *more* or *less* before the adverb.

Examples: *faster, more quickly, less quickly*

To compare three or more actions, add *-est* to the adverb, or use the words *most* or *least* before the adverb.

Examples: *fastest, most quickly, least quickly*

1. Play Tell a Tale Together with a partner.

2. Take turns adding a sentence to build a story. Choose one or more words from the chart to score points.

3. Add up the points each partner scored. Who is the winner?

(1 point each)	(2 points each)	(2 points each)
erupt	more	quickly
flow	the most	loudly
create	less	slowly
develop	the least	faster
		fastest
		sooner

Use adverbs to tell your partner another tale.

Name _____   Date _____

An Island Grows

Make an imagery chart of "An Island Grows."

Volcano	Land	Plants	Animals	People
Stone breaks. Water quakes.				

 Use your imagery chart to talk with a partner about your favorite parts of the poem.

Fluency: Intonation

An Island Grows

Use this passage to practice reading with proper intonation.

Markets sell.	2
Merchants yell.	4
"Fresh fish!"	6
"Pepper dish!"	8
"Ripe fruit!"	10
"Spicy root!"	12

© National Geographic Learning, a part of Cengage Learning, Inc.

Intonation

B ☐ Does not change pitch.   **A** ☐ Changes pitch to match some of the content.

I ☐ Changes pitch, but does not match content.   **AH** ☐ Changes pitch to match all of the content.

Accuracy and Rate Formula

Use the formula to measure a reader's accuracy and rate while reading aloud.

_____ − _____ = _____
words attempted   number of errors   words correct per minute
in one minute   (wcpm)

Name _____   Date _____

Volcano Views

Complete this chart as you read "Volcano Views."

Page	My question	The answer

 Tell a partner which answer or fact was most interesting and why.

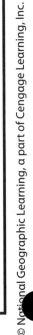

Name _____ Date _____

Compare Texts

Write details from each text. Add a star to details that are similar in both texts.

"An Island Grows"	"Volcano Views"
Tells about volcanoes under the sea	Tells about a man who photographs volcanoes
Tells about magma and lava	Tells about magma and lava

 Talk with a partner. Tell each other which text you liked better and why.

Grammar: Adverbs

Volcanoes Rock!

Grammar Rules Adverbs

Adverbs tell more about a verb.

Islands grow **slowly**. (tells how)

Some lava flows **faster** than other lava. (compares two actions)

Thick lava flows the **least quickly** of all. (compares three or more actions)

Underline the adverbs.

I am a scientist. I see volcanoes erupt. I saw one yesterday. The ground rumbled loudly. Rocks soon flew out. The lava flowed more quickly than any lava I have seen. It glowed brightly.

The lava flows more slowly today. Ash floats everywhere. It is an amazing sight!

Write three sentences about forces of nature. Use adverbs. Read your sentences to a partner.

Name _____   Date _____

Underwater Earthquakes

Make a cause-and-effect chart about underwater earthquakes.

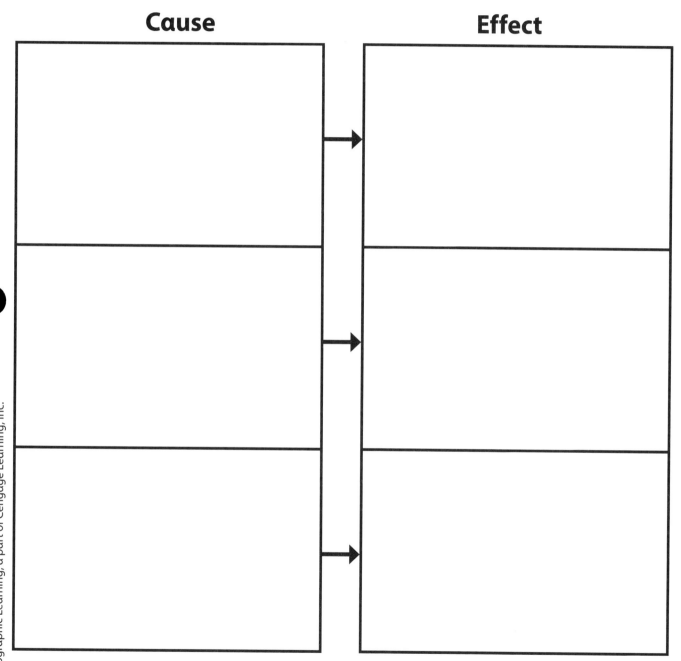

Cause	Effect

 Use your chart to tell a partner about one cause-and-effect relationship related to a tsunami.

Name _____   Date _____

On, Across, Before

Grammar Rules Prepositions

Some prepositions tell where, show direction, or show time.

Where	Direction	Time
on, near	into, from, across	before, during, after

Write a preposition from the chart to complete each sentence.

A tsunami is near, so we must drive away ____from____ the sea.

_____ the trip, Mom checks a map for the quickest way. Then

we all get _____ the car.

_____ our trip, Mom gives Dad directions. My sister sits

_____ me in the back. Soon, Dad drives _____ a bridge. We

see a town _____ the other side. _____ a short ride, we are

safe!

 Tell a partner how you could get away from a storm. Use prepositions.

Key Points Reading

Selvakumar Knew Better

1 It was a beautiful day in December. Selvakumar's human family was making breakfast, just like any other day. But Selvakumar knew something was wrong.

Suddenly, there was a loud noise. An earthquake! Big waves would soon come to shore. Selvakumar knew it. But his family did not. They needed to run to safety.

2 Papa saw the tsunami first. He told everyone to run. Mama took the two smallest boys and told Dinakaran to run up the hill. Instead, Dinakaran ran to the house.

But Selvakumar knew better. He made Dinakaran leave the house. They ran up the hill together. They were both safe.

3 After the tsunami ended, the family found each other on the hill. They hugged each other. They felt happy to be safe and alive.

They hugged Selvakumar, too, because he knew better. He saved Dinakaran's life!

Name _____   Date _____

Before an Earthquake

Grammar Rules Prepositional Phrases

A preposition often has a noun or pronoun after it. Together, these words make a prepositional phrase.
I went **to the store**.
I got a letter **from her**.

Draw a line under the prepositional phrase in each sentence.

1. Karim lives <u>near the shore</u>.

2. One day, he feels the ground shake under his feet.

3. He runs into the house and tells his mother.

4. "We must leave before the earthquake," his mother says.

5. She packs food in the kitchen.

6. She loads a backpack and puts it on Karim's back.

7. They hurry from the town.

8. They go to a safe place.

9. They stay safe during the earthquake.

10. After the earthquake, they return home.

 Talk with a partner. Decide whether each prepositional phrase tells where, shows direction, or shows time.

7.14

Selvakumar Knew Better

Make a cause-and-effect chart for "Selvakumar Knew Better."

Cause	Effect
Selvakumar hears a sound.	He whines and barks to warn his family.
Mama picks up the two youngest boys and screams for Dinakaran to follow her up the hill.	

💬 **Use your chart to tell a partner about one cause and effect you wrote about from the selection.**

Selvakumar Knew Better

Use this passage to practice reading with proper expression.

As Dinakaran and Selvakumar rested, they heard the 8
grownups talking. 10

"We'll never recover," moaned one man. 16

"We've lost absolutely everything," someone else said. 23

But Selvakumar felt the regular rhythm of Dinakaran's 31
chest rising and falling under his chin. Then he heard 41
Dinakaran's little brothers nearby. He smelled the familiar 49
scents of Papa and Mama. 54

And Selvakumar knew better. 58

Expression

B ☐ Does not read with feeling.

I ☐ Reads with some feeling, but does not match content.

A ☐ Reads with appropriate feeling for most content.

AH ☐ Reads with appropriate feeling for all content.

Accuracy and Rate Formula

Use the formula to measure a reader's accuracy and rate while reading aloud.

_____ – _____ = _____
words attempted in one minute   number of errors   words correct per minute (wcpm)

© National Geographic Learning, a part of Cengage Learning, Inc.

Name _____ Date _____

Tsunami

Complete this chart as you read "Tsunami."

K What I Know	W What I Want to Know	L What I Learned	Q Questions I Still Have

 Use your chart to tell two other classmates what you learned about tsunamis.

Name _____ Date _____

Compare Texts

Compare "Selvakumar Knew Better" and "Tsunami."

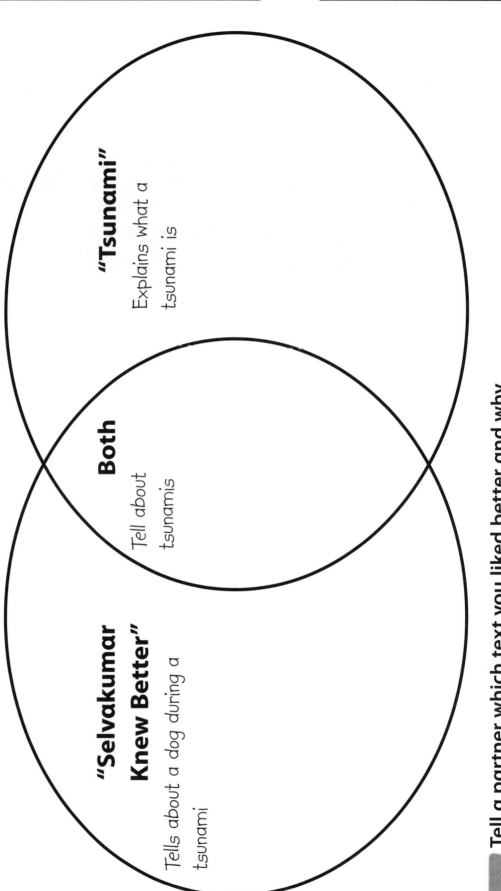

"Tsunami"

Explains what a tsunami is

Both

Tell about tsunamis

"Selvakumar Knew Better"

Tells about a dog during a tsunami

Tell a partner which text you liked better and why.

Grammar: Prepositional Phrases Game

Preposition Bingo

Grammar Rules Prepositional Phrases

Prepositional phrases:

• tell where	Jean's purse is **under the seat**.
• show direction	The man walked **into the store**.
• show time	My cat sleeps **during the day**.
• add details	Greg added some pepper **to the stew**.

Directions:

1. Write one preposition in each box: *into, on, before, after, to, across, over, under, during.*

2. Your teacher will say a sentence with a prepositional phrase. Listen for the preposition in the sentence.

3. Put an "X" in the box with that preposition.

4. Once you have a complete row, yell: *Bingo!*

5. Say another sentence that uses the preposition.

💬 **Point to a preposition in your chart. A partner uses it in a sentence.**

Selvakumar Knew Better

Setting: The play takes place at Dinakaran's house and on top of a nearby hill.

Cast of Characters: Narrator; Dinakaran; Selvakumar, the dog; Dinakaran's mother

Scene 1: At Dinakaran's house

Dinakaran is sitting on the floor of his house. He looks frightened. Selvakumar, on all fours, barks and paws at him.

Narrator: It seemed like an ordinary morning. But Selvakumar knew better. The earth was shaking. There was a roaring sound in the distance. A big tidal wave was coming, and Selvakumar knew that his friend Dinakaran was in danger.

Dinakaran: Go away, Selvakumar! I'll be safe here. Leave me alone.

Selvakumar *[growling a little]:* No, it's not safe! We have to go! We need to find your family!

Dinakaran: I'm afraid! I don't want to go!

Selvakumar pulls at Dinakaran's shirt. He tugs him toward the door.

Selvakumar *[growling louder]:* Listen to that noise! We aren't safe here – let's go!

Narrator: Finally, Dinakaran understood why Selvakumar was worried. He knew he had to run as fast as he could.

Dinakaran jumps up. He and Selvakumar run outside and offstage.

Narrator: There was a huge roar. Water covered Dinakaran's house and the whole village. Dinakaran and Selvakumar ran and ran until they got to the top of the hill. They were safe!

Scene 2: On the hill

Dinakaran's mother is standing on the hill. She runs back and forth. She looks in every direction.

Dinakaran's Mother *[shouting and crying]*: Dinakaran! Where are you?

Selvakumar and Dinakaran run toward Dinakaran's mother. They are panting and puffing. She hugs Dinakaran tightly. Selvakumar barks and runs around them.

Dinakaran's Mother: Oh, my son! You're safe!

Dinakaran *[crying]*: Mama! I wanted to stay in the house. I thought I would be safe there, but Selvakumar knew better.

Narrator: Dinakaran told his mother what Selvakumar had done. She felt very happy. She was proud of Selvakumar.

Dinakaran's mother hugs Selvakumar tightly. Selvakumar wags his tail.

Dinakaran's Mother: Thank you, Selvakumar. Thank you for saving my son!

Narrator: Then Dinakaran and his mother and the rest of Dinakaran's family hugged Selvakumar tightly. They were all safe, every one of them. It was all because Selvakumar knew better.

End of play

Name _____ Date _____

Organization

Writing is organized when it is easy to follow. All the ideas make sense together and flow from one idea to the next in an order that fits the writer's audience and purpose.

	Is the writing organized? Does it fit the audience and purpose?	Does the writing flow?
4	❑ The writing is very well-organized. ❑ It clearly fits both the writer's audience and purpose.	❑ The writing is smooth and logical. Each sentence flows into the next one.
3	❑ Most of the writing is organized. ❑ It mostly fits the writer's audience and purpose.	❑ Most of the writing is smooth. There are only a few sentences that do not flow logically.
2	❑ The writing is not well-organized. ❑ It fits the writer's audience or the writer's purpose, but not both.	❑ Some of the writing is smooth. Many sentences do not flow smoothly.
1	❑ The writing is not organized at all. ❑ It does not fit the writer's audience or purpose.	❑ The sentences do not flow smoothly or logically.

Main Idea and Details Diagram

Complete a main idea and details diagram for each paragraph of your research report.

Main Idea:
Detail:
Detail:
Detail:
Detail:
Detail:

Revise

Use the Revising Marks to revise this paragraph from a research report. As you revise, look for:

- information that has been paraphrased, not plagiarized
- smooth flow of ideas

Revising Marks	
∧	Add.
℘	Take out.
⟳	Move to here.

Tsunamis are a series of destructive sea waves caused by an

earthquake or volcanic eruption. What are tsunamis? When the waves

reach land they can be 100 feet high and cause a lot of destruction.

Tsunamis are a frequent occurrence in Japan.

Edit and Proofread

Use the Editing Marks to edit and proofread this paragraph. Look for:

- **adverbs**
- **prepositions**
- **commas in a series**
- **spelling of compound words**

Editing Marks	
∧	Add.
℘	Take out.
⟳	Move to here.
◯	Check spelling.
﹐	Add comma.

Earth is made up of layers. A crack underneath the crust causes a fault, or thin line of rock crushed between two blocks of rock. The fault can be vertical horizontal or at an angle. When the earth cracks sudden, the ground can start to shake. The earth shakes furious with the onset beside an eartquake.

Name _____ Date _____

Getting There

Make a concept map with the answers to the Big Question: What tools can we use to achieve our goals?

What tools can we use to achieve our goals?

Name _____ Date _____

The Big Race

Make a story map about a goal and outcome in life.

Goal

Events

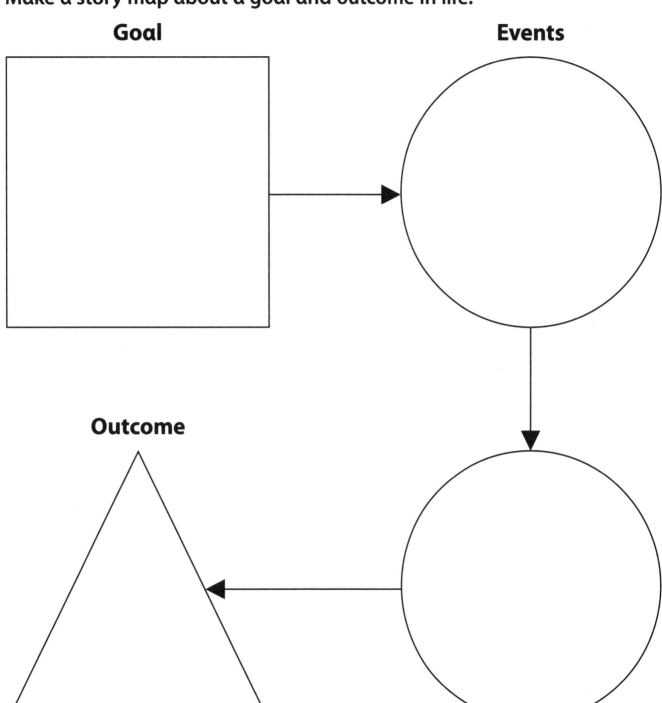

Outcome

 Talk with a partner about how each event relates to the goal and the outcome.

Grammar: Regular Past-Tense Verbs

Fun Run

Grammar Rules Regular Past-Tense Verbs

Use past-tense verbs to tell about something that already happened.

1. For most verbs, add **-ed**.

   talk → talked

2. If a verb ends in silent **e**, drop the **e** and add **-ed**.

   live → lived

3. If a one-syllable verb ends in one vowel and one consonant, double the consonant and add **-ed**.

   tap → tapped

Fill in the blanks with past-tense verbs.

My friend _____ me to go to a "fun run" with her. I _____
    (ask)   (enjoy)
it, but I had one problem. When the race _____, I _____ over
                                          (start)   (trip)
my shoelace and fell down! My friend _____ me up. Other
                                       (help)
runners _____ to see if I was okay. I _____ up and kept
         (stop)   (jump)
running. The rest of the race was fun. The runners _____ and
                                                     (laugh)
_____ during the race. When it _____, we _____ delicious
 (chat)   (end)   (share)
cookies. Yum! It was truly a fun run!

🔲 **Tell a partner about something you did last weekend.
    Use past-tense verbs.**

© National Geographic Learning, a part of Cengage Learning, Inc.

Key Points Reading

Running Shoes

Every year, the number man comes. He counts everyone in Sophy's village. One year, he sees Sophy looking at his running shoes. She wants a pair like them. They can make her wish come true.

In a month, Sophy receives a pair of running shoes in the mail.

Sophy asks her mother if she can go to school. Her mother says it is too far away. Sophy says that she has running shoes now. She can run there. Her mom smiles and tells her it is okay.

The next day, Sophy runs the whole way to school. She tells the teacher that she wants to learn to read and write. The boys laugh at her, but Sophy wins a race against all of them. They become her friends, too.

One year later, the number man comes back to Sophy's village. She tells him that her dream is to help build a school in her village and to become a teacher.

Name _____ Date _____

From Present to Past

Grammar Rules Past Tense: Irregular Verbs

Some verbs change in special ways to show an action in the past:

Now:	am/is	are	do/does	go/goes
Past:	was	were	did	went

1. Play with a partner.

2. Spin the spinner.

3. Change the present-tense verb to the past tense. Spell the past-tense form and use it in a sentence.

Make a Spinner

1. Push a brad 🖈 through the center of the spinner.

2. Open the brad on the back.

3. Hook a paper clip ▭ over the brad on the front to make a spinner.

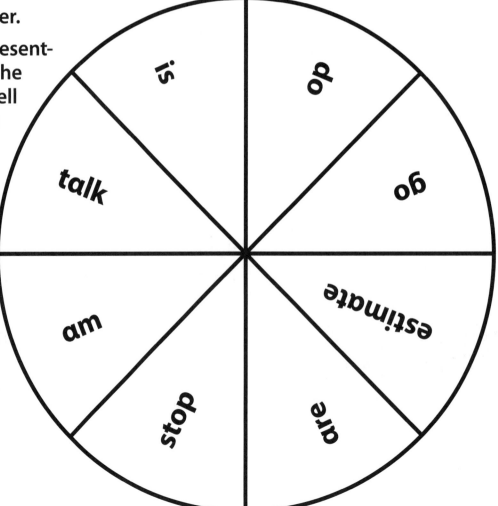

is
do
go
talk
estimate
am
stop
are

© National Geographic Learning, a part of Cengage Learning, Inc.

Reread and Summarize: Story Map

Running Shoes

Make a story map for "Running Shoes."

Goal

Sophy wants to go to school.

Events

1. The number man comes to her village.

2. He orders running shoes for Sophy.

3.

Outcome

Use your story map to talk with a partner about how Sophy achieves her goal.

Fluency: Intonation

Running Shoes

Use this passage to practice reading with proper intonation.

"Running shoes!" she yelled. She carefully put   7

on each shoe. "Now my wish will come true."   16

"What wish?" her mother asked.   21

"I want to go to school."   27

"But the school is eight kilometers away over horrible roads."   37

"Yes, but now I have running shoes!" Sophy   45

said as she bounced up and down.   52

Intonation

B ☐ Does not change pitch.   A ☐ Changes pitch to match some of the content.

I ☐ Changes pitch, but does not match content.   AH ☐ Changes pitch to match all of the content.

Accuracy and Rate Formula

Use the formula below to measure a reader's accuracy and rate while reading aloud.

_____ − _____ = _____
words attempted   number of errors   words corrected per minute
in one minute   (wcpm)

Reading Options: Prediction Chart

Two Clever Plans

Complete this chart as you read "Two Clever Plans."

What I know about the character	What I think will happen

 Talk with a partner about your predictions. Did they match the outcomes? Why or why not?

© National Geographic Learning, a part of Cengage Learning, Inc.

Name _____ Date _____

Compare Settings

Compare the settings in "Three Golden Apples" and "Turtle and His Four Cousins."

	"Three Golden Apples"	"Turtle and His Four Cousins"
Where	Greece	
When		

💬 **Talk with a partner about the stories. Tell which story character you liked best and why.**

8.9

Grammar: Present and Past Tense Verbs

After School

Grammar Rules Verb Tenses: Present and Past

Use present tense to tell about an action that happens now or happens often.

Use past tense to tell about an action that already happened.

Present tense ➔ I **run** three kilometers every day.

Past tense ➔ I **ran** three kilometers yesterday.

Fill in the blanks with present-tense or past-tense verbs.

Every day after school, I _____ soccer. Yesterday, we _____
(play)   (play)
a game. At first, I _____ nothing. I _____ on the bench.
(do)   (am)
I _____ my friends. Then the coach _____ over to me.
(watch)   (run)

"Maria," she said, "You always _____ fast. You always _____
(run)   (kick)
the ball well. We _____ you now."
(need)

I _____ out on the field. I _____ a goal! Our team _____
(go)   (score)   (is)
the winner!

 Tell a partner about something you did yesterday and something you do almost every day. Use past-tense and present-tense verbs.

8.10

Sophy's Running Shoes

Setting: The play takes place at Sophy's house and at school.

Cast of Characters: Narrator, Sophy, Sophy's Mother, Teacher

Scene 1: At Sophy's house

Sophy is standing in front of a one-room house with a thatched roof. Her feet are bare. She is holding a shoebox in her hands. Her mother stands just inside the door of the house.

Narrator: Sophy had a secret wish. The day she got a package in the mail, she knew that her wish could come true.

Sophy *[calling inside]*: Mother! Look, I got a package!

Sophy's mother steps outside.

Sophy's Mother *[curiously]*: What is it, Sophy?

Sophy opens the box in her hands. She carefully puts on the shoes.

Sophy *[excitedly]*: Running shoes! Now my wish can come true.

Sophy's Mother: What is your wish, Sophy?

Sophy: I want to go to school!

Sophy's Mother *[worried]*: But it is eight kilometers away. The roads are very bad. How will you get to school?

Sophy: I will run! I have running shoes now.

Narrator: Sophy's mother remembered how Sophy's father used to sit with her. He taught her words. But now Sophy's father was dead. There was no one to teach her.

Sophy's Mother *[smiling]*: You may go to school, Sophy.

Narrator: On her first day of school, Sophy got up very early. She ate breakfast and put on her running shoes. Then she ran and ran. She finally saw the schoolhouse.

Scene 2: At school

Sophy stands at the door of a one-room schoolhouse. There are sandals lined up next to the door. She bends down and unties her shoes. She walks quietly inside. The teacher looks at her and smiles.

Teacher: Hello. Who are you?

Sophy *[shyly]*: My name is Sophy. I want to learn to read and write.

Narrator: The other students were all boys. They laughed at Sophy. But the teacher told Sophy that she was welcome to the school.

Teacher *[kindly]*: Where are you from, Sophy? How did you get here?

Sophy: I am from Andong Kralong. I ran here this morning.

Teacher *[surprised]*: That's eight kilometers away!

Sophy *[proudly]*: Yes, Miss. But I have running shoes. And I want to learn to read and write.

Narrator: At first, school was not easy for Sophy. The boys laughed at her. But she challenged them to a race and she won. They stopped laughing. Sophy studied hard and learned many things. Then she had a new dream.

Sophy *[to audience]*: I want to build a school in my village. And I want to be the teacher.

End of play

Thinking Map: Main Idea Diagram

A Traveler's Adventure

Make a main idea diagram about the main idea: There are many interesting places to visit.

Main Idea

Details

There are many interesting places to visit.

Take turns with your partner telling other details that could support the main idea.

Grammar: Future Tense

I Will Explore the World

Grammar Rules Future Tense with *will*

To tell about an action in the future, you can use the helping verb *will* with the main verb.

Our class **will go** on a field trip next week.

Fill in the blank with the future-tense form of each underlined verb.

1. I often <u>visit</u> the children's museum. Next week I _____ a new room there.

2. In this room, you can <u>learn</u> about places around the world. I _____ about new places to explore.

3. You can <u>use</u> math to figure out how far away each place is. I _____ math to figure out the distance to Hawaii.

4. People <u>fly</u> across the Pacific Ocean to Hawaii. Someday, I _____ there, too.

5. People <u>explore</u> Hawaii's beaches and volcanoes. I _____ all of its islands.

Use three of the verbs above to tell a partner about something you will do in the future.

One Man's Goal

1

Erden Eruç has a goal. He is going to row, bike, walk, and climb around the world using his own power. He is also going to climb the highest mountain on each of six continents.

2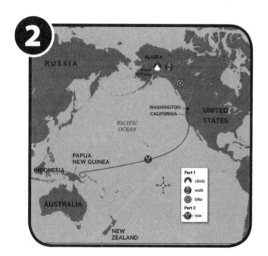

Eruç made his trip in two parts. In the first part, Eruç biked 5,546 miles from Seattle, Washington, to Mt. McKinley, Alaska. Then he climbed 20,320 feet to the top of Mt. McKinley! In the second part, he rowed alone to Australia in a small boat.

3

Eruç knows that going around the world this way is a difficult goal. But he wants to show kids that they can do great things. Even though there may be hard parts, too, kids can reach their dreams and goals.

Grammar: Future Tense

The Destination Game

Grammar Rules Future Tense with *am/is/are going to*

To tell about an action in the future, you can use *am going to*, *is going to*, or *are going to* before a main verb.

I **am going to** travel.   Pedro **is going to** travel.   Pedro and Maria **are going to** travel.

1. Play with a partner.

2. Spin the spinner.

3. Use the word or words as the subject of a sentence. Tell where each subject is going to travel or explore in the future.

Make a Spinner

1. Push a brad ⚡ through the center of the spinner.

2. Open the brad on the back.

3. Hook a paper clip ⌐⊐ over the brad on the front to make a spinner.

Reread and Summarize: Main Idea Diagram

One Man's Goal

**Make a main idea diagram for different sections
of "One Man's Goal."**

Main Idea	Details

Main Idea

Eruç decided to go around the world.

Details

He left California in a boat in 2007.

He rowed across the Pacific Ocean to Australia.

 **Use your main idea diagrams to summarize parts of the selection
for a partner.**

Fluency: Phrasing

Use this passage to practice reading with proper phrasing.

One Man's Goal

Crossing the Pacific was amazing, but that was only part of Eruç's	12
journey. He was determined to go around the world—using his own	24
energy! During his journey, Eruç wanted to climb the tallest peaks on six	37
continents to honor the memory of a fellow climber. Eruç planned to bike,	50
walk, climb, and row the world—without any motors to help him.	62

Phrasing

B ☐ Rarely pauses while reading the text.   **A** ☐ Frequently pauses at appropriate points in the text.

I ☐ Occasionally pauses while reading the text.   **AH** ☐ Consistently pauses at all appropriate points in the text.

Accuracy and Rate Formula

Use the formula to measure a reader's accuracy and rate while reading aloud.

_____	–	_____	=	_____
words attempted in one minute		number of errors		words corrected per minute (wcpm)

Reading Options: Word Detective

Climbing Toward Her Goal

Write about new words you learn as you read "Climbing Toward Her Goal."

 **Word Detective**

New Word: _____

What I think it means: _____

_____

Clues: _____

_____

Definition: _____

_____

- ✄

 Word Detective

New Word: _____

What I think it means: _____

_____

Clues: _____

_____

Definition: _____

_____

Discuss your new words with your partner. Talk about when or where you might use the word again.

© National Geographic Learning, a part of Cengage Learning, Inc.

Name _____   Date _____

Compare Causes

Compare Erden Eruç and Constanza Ceruti.

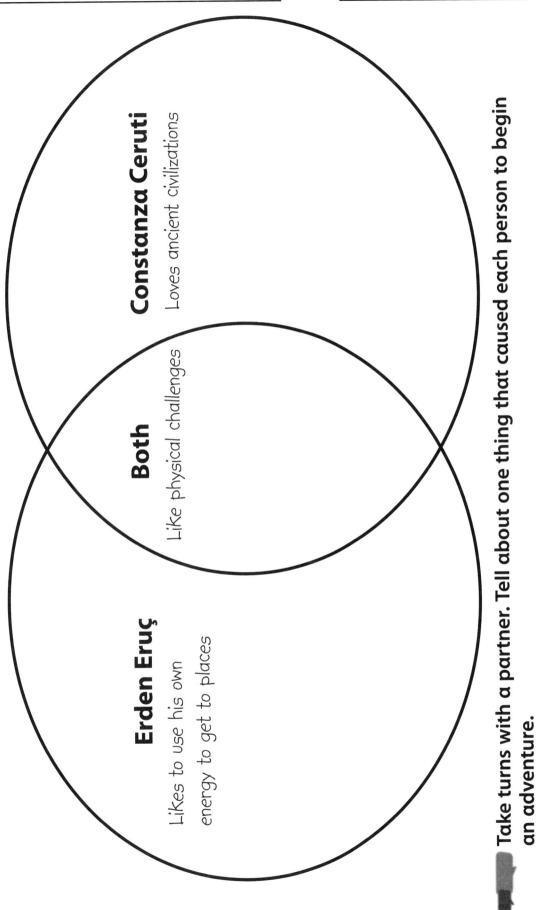

Constanza Ceruti
Loves ancient civilizations

Both
Like physical challenges

Erden Eruç
Likes to use his own energy to get to places

Take turns with a partner. Tell about one thing that caused each person to begin an adventure.

For use with TE p. T546a

8.20

Name _____   Date _____

Grammar: Future Tense with *will, am/is/are going to*

A Busy Weekend

Grammar Rules Future Tense

You can show the future tense in two different ways:

Use *will* + a main verb:	Use *am/is/are* + *going to* + a main verb:
I **will make** tacos tonight.	I **am going to make** tacos tonight.

Each sentence tells about a future action. Rewrite the verb in each sentence to show a different way to say the same thing.

1. I will study for my math test this weekend.

I _____ for my math test this weekend.

2. My sister is going to practice her basketball skills.

My sister _____ her basketball skills.

3. My brothers will prepare their science project.

My brothers _____ their science project.

4. My mother is going to help Aunt Sally move to a new home.

My mother _____ Aunt Sally move to a new home.

5. It will be a very busy weekend.

It _____ a very busy weekend.

 Tell your partner what your friends or family members will probably do this weekend. Use *will* or *going to*.

Voice

Every writer has a special way of saying things, or a voice. The voice should sound genuine, or real, and be unique to that writer.

	Does the writing sound genuine and unique ?	Does the tone fit the audience and purpose?
4	❏ The writing is genuine and unique. It shows who the writer is.	❏ The writer's tone, formal or informal, fits the audience and purpose.
3	❏ Most of the writing sounds genuine and unique.	❏ The writer's tone mostly fits the audience and purpose.
2	❏ Some of the writing sounds genuine and unique.	❏ Some of the writing fits the audience and purpose.
1	❏ The writing does not sound genuine or unique.	❏ The writer's tone does not fit the audience or purpose.

Name _____   Date _____

Story Map

Complete the story map for your story.

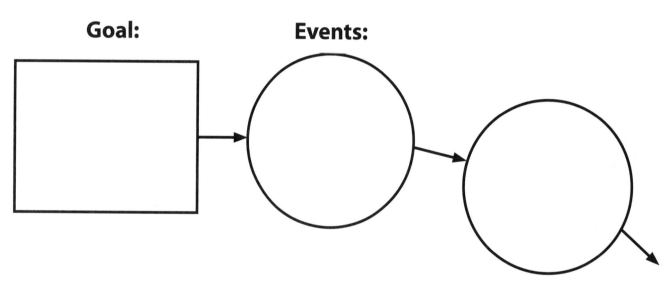

Goal: **Events:**

Writing Project

Revise

Use the Revising Marks to revise this paragraph. Look for:

- **details that tell about setting**
- **words that show personal voice**

Revising Marks	
∧	Add.
℘	Take out.

My friend Sarah loves to roller skate. She roller skates every

Saturday at the rink. Almost nothing can keep her away.

Then about a month ago, she fell and hurt her ankle really badly.

She was laid up for several weeks. One day I went to visit her.

I found her staring out a window. Without turning toward me, she

said, "I will be roller skating in a month." Knowing Sarah, I didn't

doubt her. Still, she had hurt her ankle pretty badly.

Sure enough, a month later she was there with her roller skates.

© National Geographic Learning, a part of Cengage Learning, Inc.

Writing Project

Edit and Proofread

Use the Editing Marks to edit and proofread this paragraph. Look for:

- **verb tenses**
- **punctuation with dialogue**

Editing Marks	
∧	Add.
⌿	Take out.
⸌⸍ ⸌⸍	Insert quotation marks.
⌄	Insert comma.
⊙∧	Insert period.
?∧	Insert question mark.
!∧	Insert exclamation point.

Sarah Nist the announcer called. The crowd stood up and applauds

wildly. Sarah glided onto the ice. Her left leg slided a bit as she points

her right leg straight out behind her into a graceful arabesque. The

crowd went wild again and screamed, Go Sarah Only a year ago, she

had struggled to walk after an accident. Now, she was on her way to

victory again.

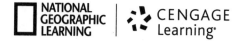

Acknowledgments

Grateful acknowledgment is given to the authors, artists, photographers, museums, publishers, and agents for permission to reprint copyrighted material. Every effort has been made to secure the appropriate permission. If any omissions have been made or if corrections are required, please contact the Publisher.

Cover Illustration: Joel Sotelo

Please see the Level D Reach Student Book for all image acknowledgments.

For product information and technology assistance, contact us at
Customer & Sales Support, 888-915-3276

For permission to use material from this text or product, submit all requests online at **www.cengage.com/permissions**
Further permissions questions can be emailed to
permissionrequest@cengage.com

National Geographic Learning | Cengage Learning
1 Lower Ragsdale Drive
Building 1, Suite 200
Monterey, CA 93940

Cengage Learning is a leading provider of customized learning solutions with office locations around the globe, including Singapore, the United Kingdom, Australia, Mexico, Brazil, and Japan. Locate your local office at **www.cengage.com/global**.

Visit National Geographic Learning online at **NGL.Cengage.com**
Visit our corporate website at **www.cengage.com**

ISBN: 978-1-3371-0991-8 (Practice Book)

ISBN: 978-1-3371-0997-0 (Practice Masters)
Teachers are authorized to reproduce the practice masters in this book in limited quantity and solely for use in their own classrooms.

Printed in the USA.
Globus Printing & Packaging, Inc.
Minster, OH

Print Number: 01

Print Year: 2016